Resilient Borders and
Cultural Diversity

New Studies of Modern Japan

Series Editors: Doug Slaymaker and William M. Tsutsui

New Studies of Modern Japan is a multidisciplinary series that consists primarily of original studies on a broad spectrum of topics dealing with Japan since the mid-nineteenth century. Additionally, the series aims to bring back into print classic works that shed new light on contemporary Japan. The series speaks to cultural studies (literature, translations, film), history, and social sciences audiences. We publish compelling works of scholarship, by both established and rising scholars in the field, on a broad arena of topics, in order to nuance our understandings of Japan and the Japanese.

Advisory Board

Titles in the Series

Haiku Poetics in Twentieth Century Avant-Garde Poetry, by Jeffrey Johnson
Literary Mischief: Sakaguchi Ango, Culture, and the War, edited by James Dorsey and Doug Slaymaker
Japan's Siberian Intervention, 1918–1922: "A Great Disobedience Against the People," edited by Paul E. Dunscomb
Truth from a Lie: Documentary, Detection, and Reflexivity in Abe Kōbō's Realist Project, by Margaret S. Key
Japan's Backroom Politics: Factions in a Multiparty Age, by Watanabe Tsuneo, Translated and with commentary by Robert D. Eldridge
Resilient Borders and Cultural Diversity: Internationalism, Brand Nationalism, and Multiculturalism in Japan, by Koichi Iwanbuchi

Resilient Borders and Cultural Diversity

Internationalism, Brand Nationalism, and Multiculturalism in Japan

Koichi Iwabuchi

LEXINGTON BOOKS
Lanham • Boulder • New York • London

Published by Lexington Books
An imprint of The Rowman & Littlefield Publishing Group, Inc.
4501 Forbes Boulevard, Suite 200, Lanham, Maryland 20706
www.rowman.com

Unit A, Whitacre Mews, 26-34 Stannary Street, London SE11 4AB

British Library Cataloguing in Publication Information Available

Library of Congress Cataloging-in-Publication Data Available

Iwabuchi, Koichi, 1960–
Resilient borders and cultural diversity : internationalism, brand nationalism, and multiculturalism in
Japan / Koichi Iwabuchi.
pages cm. — (New studies of modern Japan)
Includes bibliographical references and index.
ISBN 978-1-4985-0225-2 (cloth : alkaline paper) — ISBN 978-1-4985-0226-9 (electronic)
1. Japan—Relations. 2. Japan—Ethnic relations. 3. Multiculturalism—Japan. 4. Internationalism—
Economic aspects—Japan. 5. Nationalism—Japan. 6. Business names—Political aspects—Japan. 7.
Globalization—Political aspects—Japan. 8. Marketing—Political aspects—Japan. 9. Mass media—
Political aspects—Japan. 10. Japan—Commerce. I. Title.
DS891.2.I95 2015
303.48'252—dc23

2014047061

∞™ The paper used in this publication meets the minimum requirements of American
National Standard for Information Sciences Permanence of Paper for Printed Library
Materials, ANSI/NISO Z39.48-1992.

Printed in the United States of America

Contents

Acknowledgments

Quite often we have only a vague idea of how several studies we are conducting are linked to each other when we are in the midst of research. Only when we revisit all of the works later from a bird's-eye perspective do we come to realize a consistent theoretical concern that has pushed us throughout the investigation. This book is born from such a process. Since the mid-1990s, I have been fascinated with the examination of trans-Asian media culture connection, which is uneven but has great potential for fostering cross-border dialogue. Preparation for producing this book has offered me a great chance to clearly shape my ideas for the research I have been conducting for the last ten years or so, after the publication of my first book, regarding an intricate intersection of the intensification of media culture globalization and that of multicultural questions. I could elucidate a sense, which has been gradually prevailing within my mind, that an "international" perspective subtly governs cross-border connectivity and dialogue, cultural diversity within and across national borders, as well as my understanding of the phenomenon in a restrictive manner. Also, I have been sharply reminded once again that border transgression is persistently a key issue for my research as well as my way of life and how it is arduous to achieve. So my small, everlasting challenge goes on!

As always, so many people implicitly and explicitly helped my research and writing. I would especially like to thank the following people for various reasons, such as giving me valuable insights and constructive encouragement; offering me great research occasions for presentation and publication; and sharing stimulating dialogue, intellectual excitement, and fun: Ien Ang, Chris Berry, Eddie Kuo Chen-Yu, Leo Ching, Chua Beng Huat, Yiu Fai Chow, Jeroen de Kloet, John Erni, Anthony Fung, Ulf Hannerz, Ariel Heryanto, Mette Hjort, Mark Hobart, Shuhei Hosokawa, Kelly Hu, Mamoru Ito,

Michael Keane, Olivia Khoo, Kim Hyun Mee, Kim Youna, Lee Dong-Hoo, Nichola Liscutin, Jacquie Lo, Fran Martin, Yoshitaka Mori, Meaghan Morris, Tessa Morris-Suzuki, Shinji Oyama, Eva Tsai, Daya Thussu, Graeme Turner, Shoji Yamada, Tomiko Yoda, and Audrey Yue. Many thanks also go to all the students with whom I have shared a great deal of time in the classroom at various universities in many different countries and cities. While some parts of the research were conducted while I was teaching at the International Christian University and Waseda University in Tokyo, a productive research environment at Monash University enabled me to complete this book. I would especially like to thank Rae Frances, dean of the arts faculty of Monash University, for her support for my current position, as well as all the colleagues who are involved in the activities of Monash Asia Institute for their inspiring and joyful company. I am also grateful to Brighid Klick, Brian Hill, and Joseph Miller of Lexington Books for their great editorial care.

Some parts of the chapters were included in the following journals and edited volumes, although all of the previous works have been revised, edited, updated, and restructured to fit the theme of this book: "Against Banal Internationalism," *Asian Journal of Social Science* 41 (2014): 437–52 (chapter 1); "Uses of Media Culture, Usefulness of Media Culture Studies: Beyond Brand Nationalism into Public Dialogue," in *Creativity and Academic Activism: Instituting Cultural Studies*, ed. Meaghan Morris and Mette Hjort (Durham, NC: Duke University Press; Hong Kong: Hong Kong University Press, 2012), 139–56 (chapter 2); "Lost in TransNation: Tokyo and the Urban Imaginary in the Era of Globalization," *Inter-Asia Cultural Studies* 9, no. 4 (2008): 543–56 (chapter 3); "Globalization, East Asian Media Cultures and Their Publics," in "Asian Communication Research: The Past 20 Years, and the Next," special issue, *Asian Journal of Communication* 20, no. 2 (2010): 197–212 (chapters 3 and 6); "Multinationalizing the Multicultural: The Commodification of 'Ordinary Foreign Residents' in a Japanese TV Talk Show," *Japanese Studies* 25, no. 2 (September 2005): 103–18 (chapter 4); "'Ordinary Foreigners' Wanted: Multinationalization of Multicultural Questions in a Japanese TV Talk Show," in *Television, Japan, and Globalization*, ed. Mitsuhiro Yoshimoto, Eva Tsai, and Jung Bong Choi (Ann Arbor: Center for Japanese Studies, University of Michigan, 2010), 27–50 (chapter 4); "When Korean Wave Meets Resident Koreans in Japan," in *East Asian Pop Culture: Approaching the Korean Wave*, ed. Beng Huat Chua and Koichi Iwabuchi (Hong Kong: Hong Kong University Press, 2008), 243–64 (chapter 5); "De-Westernization, Inter-Asian Referencing and Beyond," *European Journal of Cultural Studies* 16, no. 6 (2014): 44–57 (chapter 6 and conclusion). I would like to thank the editors and the publishers for their permission to make use of the above materials.

Finally, my greatest thanks go to Lina, for spending enjoyable time together, and to Michiyo, for her constant, warmest support for my life.

Koichi Iwabuchi
Melbourne, Australia, February 2015

Introduction

Media and Cultural Globalization and National Border Transgression

In the last two decades, media and cultural globalization has been considerably advanced. This has been pushed forward by complex factors such as the improvement of media culture production capacity and the growth of media culture markets in many parts of the world in the post–Cold War context, the progression of international alliance and linkage among media and cultural industries and creators, and the advancement of digital communication technologies that facilitate the above developments, including the sweeping expansion of the Internet and social media, which accelerates people's cross-border communication. These have drastically displaced the hitherto overriding division between producer and consumer, professional practices and grassroots creativities, public and private, and the sense of being here and over there. Traversing the world, numerous kinds of media culture, information, and commentary are (co)produced, circulated, consumed, mixed, and remade, which facilitate mediated connection at a distance in an unprecedented manner. Accordingly, notions such as hybridization, deterritorialization, and transnationalism have drawn our attention to cross-border interaction, fusion, and mobility, which seriously put the clearly demarcated national cultural borders into question.

Such arguments, which underline how active cultural mixing processes bring about unexpected outcomes locally, are often criticized for their optimistic construction of a "myth" of global interconnectivity by neglecting the unevenness generated by the marketization of culture and the political economy of the media culture production process (e.g., Sparks 2007; Hafez 2007). While this critique is valid, and an equivalent level of attention needs to be

1

paid to the restricting forces of globalization, it should not dismiss the progressive development of cross-border interconnection. Rather, what is required is to examine the complicated interaction between progressive possibilities and their limits articulated in the globalization process, which has manifold and contradictory consequences. One way to understand such complexity is to consider how seemingly contradictory vectors of globalizing forces—decentering–recentering, diversifying–homogenizing, and transnationalizing–nationalizing—are working simultaneously and interconstitutively. Media culture globalization has decentered the capitalist modernity from the West and the global cultural power structure from the United States, as evinced by the dynamic localization practices and the rise of non-Western media culture, including those of Japan (e.g., Tomlinson 1997). Yet this also has accompanied the restructuring of global cultural power through the web of corporate alliances and market integration taking place in many parts of the world. Jim McGuigan (2009) argues how "cool capitalism," which gives priority to individual consumer sovereignty in a profound marketization logic, is capable of subtly taking in its critique to promote further commercialization. To apply his point more extensively, capital is flexible enough to absorb subversive and opposing challenges for its own benefit.

The elastic exploitation of the emerging countertrend is also shown by the ways that globalization constantly engenders and organizes cultural diversity (Hall 1991; Hannerz 1996). This process is facilitated through globally shared cultural formats such as production technique, genre, representation style, and current youth culture trends. Arguably, many of them have been initially developed in the American production of media culture (Morley and Robins 1995), but, as shown by the prevalence of the television format business and film remaking, other players in Europe, Asia, and Latin America also contribute a great deal to enriching the repertoire of cultural formats. The world is becoming more diverse through standardization and more standardized through diversification. And this dynamic is first and foremost organized and promoted by the marketing forces operated by local and transnational media culture industries in many parts of the world.

Working together with these market-driven forces, the intensification of cross-border flows and connections do not fully displace national borders but also work to rehighlight them (e.g., Hannerz 1996; Smith 2001). The acceleration of globalization processes undoubtedly prompts cross-border flows and circulations of capital, commodities, media, and people and proliferates transnational organizations and institutions that promote such moves. While national borders continue to become more and more porous, the measures of border control are constantly reformulated to tame disordered flows and tightly redemarcate the borders—materially, physically, symbolically, and imaginatively. The intensifying cross-border flows of media culture have undeniably promoted cross-fertilization and people's cross-border exchange beyond the confinement of national borders, but not all of them lead to making a substantial transformation to an exclusive form of national identity or foster a cosmopolitan outlook in terms of openness, togetherness, and dialogue within and beyond national borders. Border crossing does not necessarily bring about the transgression of borders. Transgression of borders requires one to fundamentally question how borders in their existing form have been sociohistorically constructed and also seek to displace their exclusionary power that unevenly divides "us" and "them" as well as "here" and "there." However, the border crossing of media culture is more often than not promoted and experienced, while being dissociated from actions of transgression, and the border management subtly adjusts itself to a new geocultural configuration to maintain and even reinforce the exclusionary formation of national cultural borders.

This book examines how the evolution of market-driven cultural globalization makes the operational force of such national cultural border administration stronger in the new millennium Japanese and East Asian contexts. My particular concern is how the advancement of cross-border circulation of media culture is linked to the containment of Japan's growing multicultural situations and cross-border dialogue. The promotion of border crossing of media culture and the management of people's border-crossing movement and accompanied cultural diversity within the nation appear to be unrelated to each other or disjunctive (Appadurai 1996). However, I would argue that the two conjunctively constitute the administration of Japan's national cultural border. Cross-border media and cultural connections are more often administered in ways to strengthen a national thinking and feeling and fortify national cultural borders in a mutually exclusive manner. This development has not only accompanied but has been made possible by discouraging cross-border dialogue and the engagement with multicultural diversity within Japan. The containment of cultural diversity within national borders and the international promotion of national media culture are two sides of the same coin.

This is not to underestimate how transgressive actions and collaborations have been growing in Japan as media culture globalization has facilitated the expression and sharing of alternative views and hitherto marginalized voices, the cultivation of self-reflexivity and open-minded dialogue, and the formation of cross-border alliances. Along with many researchers, I have been looking to such progressive possibilities to get over the exclusive demarcation of national and cultural boundaries in the Japanese context and with an attention to media and cultural connections in East Asia. However, the transgressive drive of media culture globalization is never free from the strong nationalizing force of desperately seeking to redemarcate and control borders, and such re-nationalizing gravity is resilient and flexible enough to overpower such radical possibilities in Japan. Annabelle Sreberny-Mohammadi's (1991) argument, made more than twenty years ago, that the framework of the nation-state both as a spatially controlled entity and as a discursively articulated geography is of much relevance to the analysis of media globalization is even more pressing as international exchanges via media culture have become much more intensified and really an integral part of people's mundane experiences. Critical analysis of this development is a vital matter if we are to seriously consider how to make Japan's national cultural borders more inclusive and dialogic.

INTER-NATIONAL ADMINISTRATION OF CULTURAL DIVERSITY

The key approach of this book is the examination of how the advancement of market-driven media culture globalization has shaped "the inter-national administration of cultural diversity," which promotes embracing a particular kind of cross-border connectivity and exchange while suppressing others—the hyphen is placed between "inter" and "national" to underscore the reworking and strengthening of the national in tandem with the intensification of media culture globalization. Chapter 1 discusses how the inter-national administration of cultural diversity is generated through the interplay between the upsurge of global cultural interchanges and the states' growing policy interest in nation branding via the promotion of media cultures.

We have observed two significant interrelated developments regarding media culture globalization in the last twenty years: a substantial increase in global cultural events, showcases, and spectacles and the growing interest in nation branding. Their interaction facilitates the media culture of the nation-states being circulated, competitive, consumed, and branded in an international arena (Urry 2003) and makes the nation function as one of the most marketable localities of glocalization, a unit of commercialized and standardized cultural diversity that is to be promoted. Furthermore, this interaction also prompts people to experience such exchanges in such a way as to accentuate the cardinal existence of clearly delimited national cultural borders. Although this way of constructing national identity in tandem with internationalism is always a significant part of modern nation-state building, a market-driven mode of industry-state alliance for the global promotion of media cultures makes national thinking and feeling even more pervasive in the world at large as it engenders "banal inter-nationalism," which permeates the idea of the nation as the unit for global cultural exchange, competition, and diversity.

The pervasion of such an idea about the nation needs to be critically considered, for it deters us from attending to various sociocultural differences within the nation and disavows their existence as constitutive of the nation. It redemarcates and resolidifies national cultural borders, generating an essentialist reassertion of what constitutes national culture and who has the ownership of national culture, as well as enhancing the sense of national attachment among the members of the nation observing the performance of "our" culture in the world. This has a serious implication for the recognition of cultural diversity within the nation. The inter-national administration of cultural diversity has been widely instituted at the expense of ensuring neglected voices are expressed and heard in the public space and giving due recognition to marginalized subjects as full members of the national society.

Subsequent chapters analyze how the inter-national administration of cultural diversity has discouraged engagement with cross-border dialogue and multicultural questions in Japan by referring to the relevant developments of culture globalization in the Japanese and East Asian contexts. Chapter 2 focuses on the rise of a series of cultural policy discussions and implementations such as soft power, cultural/public diplomacy, and creative industries with an umbrella notion of "Cool Japan," which aims to promote nation branding via the international circulation of media culture for enhancing national interests. A prominent facet of media culture globalization in the Japanese context is the spread and favorable reception of Japanese media culture throughout the world, as seen with animation, comic books, video games, cute characters, cosplay, and films. It has certainly made the perception of Japan as a faceless economic power an old story. While this change can be seen as a corrective to the underevaluation of cultural creativity that has been developed in the Japanese society, the pendulum seems to be swinging to the other pole of celebratory discourse, which also has accompanied a serious policy interest in the further promotion of Japanese media culture in the global markets. In the last decades or two, service, information, and entertainment sectors have become a sizeable part of the global economy. Accordingly, the development of soft power, creative industries, and cultural/public diplomacy has become a significant matter for state policy. Increasing international rivalry urges the Japanese government to advance such cultural policies and, accordingly, develop an instrumental view on the uses of media culture for national interests. It can be called "brand nationalism" since, I argue, the development of such cultural policy has exercised a strong ideological function in that its narrowly focused national interests work in ways to suppress engagement with significant cultural issues of public interest, such as the structured unevenness in global media culture production, the advancement of cross-border dialogue in East Asia, and engagement with multicultural situations in Japan.

CONTAINING MULTICULTURAL QUESTIONS

Chapters 3 and 4 examine the mutually exclusive way in which the interplay of banal inter-nationalism and brand nationalism administer national cultural borders, suppressing and marginalizing multicultural questions in Japan. While the rise of Japanese media culture in the global markets is apparently a testimony of the decentralizing trends against U.S.-dominated media culture globalization, at the same time, as the worldwide distribution of Pokémon and Miyazaki animations verifies, the globalization of Japanese media culture has been underpinned by the stepping up of transnational partnerships and other forms of cooperation among media corporations based in developed countries, principally the United States. The profitability of non-Western markets and the rise of non-Western production capacity has urged American as well as other global players to collaborate with non-Western counterparts (as in the case of Pokémon, see Iwabuchi 2004b). This trend is also shown through Hollywood's Asian turn in its internationalizing endeavor of film production with the expanding markets and production capacities of Asian countries. It is arguable that America still occupies a central position in this venture in which Asian counterparts are actively cooperating, but the global cultural power relations have become more intricate. This is especially true regarding the Asia-inflected Hollywood representation of "Asia" and "Japan." Chapter 3 examines the representation of Japan in *Lost in Translation* (2003) and Japanese reactions to the film in order to consider how it both evades a classic Orientalist imagination of Japan and newly engenders international othering in the globalizing context that Japan and its modernity have lost a "unique" position vis-à-vis the West, which has long been the source of Japan's complicit comprising of the Western imaginary in the construction of an essentialist discourse of Japanese national culture (Iwabuchi 1994). However, the international complicity between America and Japan has not ended. It still operates in the emergent global cultural economy to suppress the existing multicultural reality in Japan as well as hyphenated subjects in the United States, for whom the Hollywood representation of Japan (and Asia) has a more immediate and devastating relevance to their experience of marginalization.

While chapter 3 shows how the cultural dynamic of decentering and recentering processes of media culture globalization suppress cultural diversity within national borders, chapter 4 analyzes how the latter is socially recognized and represented in the framework of banal inter-nationalism. The increasing number of foreign nationals living in Japan and the growing multicultural situations are also important facets of the Japanese experiences of globalization. While the Japanese media still fail to reflect the diverse components of the population in the process of production and representation, there have been some occasions that allow hitherto marginalized voices to express themselves in the mediated public sphere, though only in a way to redemarcate a Japanese-foreigner binary. Examining a popular TV talk show, chapter 5 discusses how the multicultural reality of Japan is represented as an Olympic-like multinational spectacle where the complexity of lives, experiences, and the sense of belonging of people from diverse cultural and ethnic backgrounds are simplified and suppressed as they are reduced to "foreigners" who will never be full members of Japanese society. While the talk show gives these individuals a precious occasion to make themselves visible and express their voices in public, they are only allowed to do this as long as they perform their assigned role of confirming Japan's national cultural borders in the face of the perceived "threat" of growing multicultural situations induced by globalization processes.

EAST ASIAN MEDIA AND CULTURAL CONNECTION AND ITS DIALOGIC POTENTIALS

Chapters 5 and 6 will discuss another eminent trend of media culture globalization regarding Japan: the rise of inter-Asian connections. In addition to animation, comic books, and cute characters, Asian markets have been very receptive to other kinds of Japanese media culture, such as TV dramas, popular music, and pop idols. At the same time, the media cultures of East Asian countries such as South Korea, Hong Kong, and Taiwan have also been circulating in the region, and inter-Asian media culture flows and connections have become a mundane experience in East Asia. Japan too has received media culture from other parts of East Asia, especially from South Korea. Through the examination of the rise of South Korean media culture in Japan, chapter 5 analyzes how inter-Asian media and cultural connections intersect the multicultural questions in Japan and how the inter-national administration of cultural diversity operates in it.

South Korean media cultures have significantly changed the image of South Korea in Japan. It is a clear testimony to how inter-Asian media and cultural connections have induced self-reflexive views among the people who consume the media cultures of other parts of East Asia. While this has accompanied improving images of and attention to resident Koreans in Japan to some extent, whether it has accompanied the understanding of their historically constituted existence and experience of discrimination is debatable. An ahistorical confusion of people and culture in the present South Korea and those of resident Koreans in Japan is still discernible, which is apt to engender the recognition of resident Koreans in Japan, who have been born and brought up in Japan, as people who belong to South Korea. This raises a question of how the rise of the culture of a "home" country has bearing on the recognition of diasporas and migrants in the host country beyond "being in but not of 'our' society."

Chapter 6 further considers the transgressive possibilities of cross-border dialogue offered by the rise of East Asian media and cultural connections as well as the limits posed by inter-nationalizing forces. By engaging the notion of inter-Asian referencing, I argue that East Asian media and cultural connections have not merely urged us to move forward the project of de-Westernized production of knowledge. Critical studies of East Asian media and cultural connections are significant not only for academic conceptualization and theorization; more significantly, inter-Asian referencing via media culture has become a mundane practice of cross-border dialogue in which people of various locales self-reflexively rethink their lives, societies, and the histories of the nation and the regions they live in, as chapter 5 discusses in the case of the Japanese reception of South Korean media culture. Revisiting the development of cross-border dialogue and its transgressive potential to go beyond the exclusionary formations of national cultural borders, I discuss some serious constraints that deter the dialogue from further advancing and suggest the necessity of studying East Asian media and cultural connections with an aim to critically engage with them and further make the best of the dialogic potentials of inter-Asian referencing as a mundane practice.

In the concluding chapter, I suggest some directions critical researchers of media and cultural globalization could take to tackle the robust forces of the inter-national administration of cultural diversity. Needless to say, the analyses that this book makes in the Japanese context cannot be generally applied to other parts of the world, but the issues that I deal with in the previous chapters are widely shared as they have been generated under globalization processes. My suggestion is thus not a concrete remedy for the case of Japan, but is made from a transnational perspective toward the progression of already existing transgressive capabilities of cross-border connections and dialogue to the full, which have been growing through the advancement of media and cultural globalization processes. It is a call for collaboration beyond borders and divides, involving various social actors outside academia, without which we cannot effectively and steadily engage with the reformulation of the resilience of exclusionary national cultural borders.

Chapter One

Banal Inter-nationalism
and Its Others

It is often argued that while the nation-state is still by far the most important governmental body, the national framework is no longer able to adequately handle the complex matters of transnational flows of capital, media, and people, so much so that "territoriality is fast becoming an anachronistic delimitation of material functions and cultural identities" (Benhabib 2002, 180). However, even if analytically verifying the limit of nation-centered thinking, researchers should not give up paying critical attention to the "anachronistic" perspective as it does not recede but hangs around by working closely with cultural globalization processes. It is undeniable that the circulation of media culture discounts national boundaries and activates transnational connections and cross-border dialogue. Yet in reality such developments have also made the national framework even more robust. This chapter discusses how this occurs with the increasing pervasiveness of the inter-nationalized modes of promotion, circulation, and consumption of media cultures. Revisiting the critique of "methodological nationalism" in the current situation, this chapter discusses how its underlying tenet has been reinforced and instituted by the synergism of the process of cultural glocalization and the upswing of nation branding that endorses it. What has been engendered in this process is "banal inter-nationalism"; a container model of the nation is further instituted as the inter-nationalized circulation and encounter of media culture has become a site in which national identity is mundanely invoked, performed, and experienced. Banal inter-nationalism is a significant issue that should receive our critical attention, for it suppresses and marginalizes multicultural questions within the nation as national cultural borders are mutually reconstituted through the process in which cross-border cultural flows and encounters are promoted in such a way as to accentuate an inter-nationalized form of cultural diversity.

METHODOLOGICAL NATIONALISM
AND GLOBALIZATION

Methodological nationalism has been criticized in social science for its taken-for-granted assumption of the nation-state as the unambiguous unit of analysis, but it has attracted renewed attention in the studies of globalization. Its main problem is the presumption of "the self-evidence of a world ordered into nation-states" and "the apparent naturalness and givenness of a world divided into societies along the lines of nation-state" (Wimmer and Schiller 2002, 303). Ulrich Beck (2006) also elaborates on the problems of methodological nationalism in relation to globalization and cosmopolitanism.[1] Beck argues that the subordination of society to the state uncritically presumes a "container model" of mutually delimiting national societies, which is derived from "a territorial understanding of society based upon state-constructed and state-controlled borders" (2006, 27). This problem persists in the analysis of globalization as the presumption of a mutually constitutive dichotomy of the national and the international, which makes one apt to take "the global as the maximum intensification of the national" (2006, 29).

In line with this argument, Andreas Hepp and Nick Couldry (2009) critically discuss the limit of nation-centered approaches in the comparative studies of international media communication. While they do not use the term *methodological nationalism*, they disapprove of "container thinking," which endures in media and communication studies and prompts a search for "national-territorial" differences and interactions of media cultures. As they rightly argue, such a model is problematic as it tends to "essentialize(s) the relation between state, (political) media system, media market and media culture into a model of binary comparison" (2009, 37). They acknowledge the lingering relevance of state power to regulate the national media system and market but call renewed attention to the reality that production and consumption of media cultures are always subject to "trans-local" processes that go beyond the nation-state framework. They propose a "transcultural approach" that analyses the process of cultural thickening "in the frame of an increasingly global communicative connectivity" (2009, 41). They do not suggest that cultural deterritorialization has made national territoriality totally irrelevant but argue that "the borders of the 'cultural thickenings' to which we belong do not necessarily correspond with territorial borders, even though territories continue to have a high relevance as a reference point for constructing national community" (2009, 39). They are concerned with the interplay between territorialization and deterritorialization, more precisely between (territorialized) specific processes of meaning articulation and (deterritorialized) generation of cultural forms "in its production and reference point" (2009, 42). The point is thus not just about a localized interpretation but about the transnationalized complexity of cultural thickening under the force of globalization. While the national is still relevant to the contextualized articulation of meanings out of transnationally circulating cultural forms, the "distinctiveness" of the national is rearticulated not in reaction to but only in tandem with cross-border cultural connection and globally shared cultural references and forms.

Hepp and Couldry's argument makes an important point about the limit of a nation-centered container model for the analysis of media culture globalization. Yet, I suggest that it is also the case that national cultures are reconstructed and articulated through globally shared cultural forms and transnational connectivity; namely, we need to consider whether and how deterritorialized cultural thickening is facilitated and structured in an international communicative arena in such a way as to further prompt a territorialized conception of the nation rather than dismantling it. This is to take the operation of the national framework seriously in the examination of cultural thickening by understanding the nation as a globally shared cultural form through which local distinctiveness and differences are expressed to each other, as will be discussed in the next section. It is my contention that a container model of the nation both has been put forward by and has orchestrated global production and circulation of culture, and this has made some impact on people's understanding and experience of global cultural encounter.

In this respect, Beck (2006, 24) makes an important distinction between methodological nationalism and national outlook, which is the subscription of social actors to the notion of methodological nationalism. Researchers might have theoretically refuted the problem of methodological nationalism for the comprehensive analysis of cultural globalization processes, but national outlook is becoming even stronger and more pervasive in people's everyday lives. It has been deeply instilled in mainstream discourses, media representations, and everyday practices of cross-border cultural exchange in which the inter-nationalized production, circulation, regulation, and consumption of media cultures play a significant role. This further advances a long-held complicit working of the national and the international to widely engender an idea of the nation as the unit of global cultural encounters. This has a highly problematical implication in the enforcement of the nation's exclusionary politics. Before elaborating on this, however, I consider more in depth the institutionalization of inter-nationalized media and cultural connectivity that sustains the permeation of national outlook.

INSTITUTIONALIZATION OF THE "NATIONAL" AS A CONSTITUENT FORM OF GLOBALIZATION

Since the 1990s, it has been widely argued that market-driven globalization does not simply homogenize the world but heterogenizes it and even generates and organizes cultural diversity (e.g., Hannerz 1996). As for media culture, this cultural dynamic occurs at the site of production as well as consumption. Globally circulating cultural products and images are consumed differently in the specific political, economic, and social contexts of each locality and by people of various sociocultural backgrounds in terms of gender, sexuality, race/ethnicity, class, and age. At the same time, in each locality these products and images are reconfigured and mixed with local elements, resulting in the creation of new products that are not merely replicas of the original. And media and cultural producers are aware of this dynamic of the localization process, so much so that "local" taste and specificity assumed as such have been incorporated into their marketing strategy of "glocalization" (Robertson 1995). Transnational corporations based in developed countries pursue profits by tailoring glocal cultures in every corner of the world's markets through transnational tie-ups and partnerships. But the significance of glocalization is not limited to a business concern, it extends to the manners in which a particular kind of diversity is promoted on a globally common ground. American and Western cultural influences are always and already inscribed in the formation of media cultures in many parts of the world, but this inscription has become even deeper and more structural in the last few decades. The new configuration of cultural power exploits the locally specific meaning construction process in a globally tailored manner. Glocalization generates an entangled interplay of standardization and diversification whereby, as Richard Wilk (1995, 118) argues, cultural difference is expressed and highlighted "in ways that are more widely intelligible" through "universal categories and standards by which all cultural differences can be defined." Especially important for the generation of a "structure of common difference" is the global diffusion and sharing of cultural formats such as narrative style, visual representation, digitalized special effects, marketing technique, and the idea of coolness—most of which "originate" in the United States and other developed countries—through which various differences are articulated in the international arena.

Cultural specificity or particularity being articulated through a common or universal form is a long-standing feature of the modern era. As Roland Robertson (1995, 36) points out, it was during the nineteenth and early twentieth centuries that "'the world' became locked into a particular form of a strong shift to unicity" through "the organized attempts to link localities on an international or ecumenical basis." While the locality can take various forms, ranging from a small community to a transnational regional community, it is "the national" that has become a "prototype of the particular," a container form in which cultural specificity is articulated through common cultural formats:

> Much of the apparatus of contemporary nations, of the national-state organization of societies, including *the form* of their particularities—the construction of their unique identities—is very similar across the entire world. (Robertson 1995, 34)

Thus, the nation has long been functioning as the most prominent local unit of cultural diversity, a globally shared cultural form though which cultural distinctiveness is expressed and recognized in the international community via common cultural formats.

However, especially since early 1990s after the end of Cold War, the market-oriented process of cultural globalization has been furthering this momentum on a global scale. The key players of this process include international organizations such as the United Nations Educational, Scientific and Cultural Organization (UNESCO) and International Olympic Committee (IOC) and, more significantly, media and cultural industries that transnationally and locally work with/for such organizations. In the last two decades, the number of occasions of international media spectacle and cultural exhibition and festival has increased substantially, as seen in sports events, film festivals, TV/music awards, food expos, pageants, and tourism, as well as the proliferation of satellite and cable broadcasting and audio-visual Internet sites. These constitute what John Urry (2003, 87) calls "global screen," a site through which "localities, cultures and nations appear, to compete and to mobilize themselves as spectacles." In this process, the specificity of a nation has been "increasingly consumed by others, compared and evaluated, and turned into a brand" (Urry 2003, 107). What is crucial here is that the national has functioned as one of the most profitable local markets, as a unit of commercialized cultural diversity in the world, whereby the images of the nation have become more and more constituted as a brand through global mass cultural formats. Global mass cultural formats do not just provide the basis for the expression of national cultural distinctiveness but also work as an inter-nationalized interface that highlights the specific nationality of cultures and, as I discuss later, propagates the idea of the nation as the unit of global cultural encounters in which people are urged to participate.

GLOBALIZATION OF SOFT POWER
AND NATION BRANDING

This development makes Urry apt to say that "the nation has become something of a free-floating signifier relatively detached from the 'state' within

the swirling contours of the new global order" (2003, 87). However, internationally orchestrated cultural globalization processes have engendered increasing interest in the enhancement of the nation's image as a brand, and the
states have become rather keen to take an initiative by joining forces with
media and cultural industries. The management of the nation's image in the
world is an old story, but it has been developing into "a strategically planned,
holistic and coherent activity" by incorporating marketing techniques since
the late 1990s; British brand consultant Simon Anholt allegedly coined the
term *nation branding* in 1996 (Szondi 2008, 4). The international improvement of a nation's brand images via the circulation of media culture has been
widely regarded as a serious business through which states enhance national
interests in terms of economy and foreign policy.

The policy concern of nation branding has been widely discussed in relation to creative industries and cultural/public diplomacy, but *soft power* is the
term most often used in Japan as well as in other East Asian countries. The
term *soft power* was first coined by American political scientist Joseph Nye.
In 1990, Nye argued that "soft co-optic power" was a significant factor in the
attainment of global hegemony by the United States; he defines this as the
power to get "others to want what you want" through such symbolic resources as media and consumer culture: "If [a dominant country's] culture
and ideology are attractive, others will more willingly follow" (32). The
United States' use of media culture for advancing public diplomacy is nothing new. Indeed, the U.S. policy of disseminating the image of liberty, afflu-
ence, and democracy through media and consumer culture in order to win the
Cold War is all too well known. However, Nye considered it imperative in
the post–Cold War context that the U.S. government further develop a soft
power policy, the point being to make strategic use of a globally diffused
media and consumer culture, of symbolic icons and positive images and
values associated with the United States. A decade later, the concept of soft
power attracted renewed attention in the context of the Bush administration's
hard-line policies, especially after 9/11. But the discussion of soft power was
also extended to other parts of the world. The next chapter discusses in detail
the rise of such cultural policy discourses in Japan, but it should be noted that
Japan's soft power turn is symptomatic of the globalization of soft power.

In the last two decades, many countries other than the United States have
significantly developed the capacity to produce media cultural texts and symbolic images thanks to the development of digital communication technologies and globally adoptable cultural formats, as well as the expansion of
media culture markets in previously less developed regions. While Nye de-
plored the decline of American soft power under the Bush administration,
other states began to pursue more aggressively the idea of exploiting the
economic and political utility of media culture in order to win the international competition, although the term *soft power* was not necessarily used.

"Cool Britannia" might be the best-known policy and practice of this kind, but in East Asia as well, South Korea, Singapore, China, Taiwan, and Japan are keen to promote their own cultural products and industries in order to enhance political and economic national interests. Most famously, the South Korean government has actively promoted its media cultures overseas since the 1990s, thereby contributing to the sweeping popularity of South Korean media cultures, known as the Korean Wave. The Korean success has done a great deal to stimulate neighboring countries to seriously develop cultural policy in order to boost their nation's soft power. Indeed "soft power competition" has been intensifying in twenty-first century East Asia (Chua 2012).

While media culture is now publicly recognized as a useful resource for promoting political and economic national interests, the internationalization of soft power does in fact diverge from Nye's original argument in significant respects. One such divergence has to do with the uses of media culture as a resource in the context of international image politics. According to Nye (2004), media culture is just one of three possible resources for the enhancement of a nation's soft power, the other two being respectful foreign policy and attractive democratic values established in the relevant society. In particular, Nye clearly warns against conflating the international appeal of media cultures with soft power, stressing that soft power will not be enhanced if the other two resources are not properly developed. What is striking, however, is that this kind of conflation is actually a prevalent operational principle of cultural policy discussions in many parts of the world. Main players, it turns out, are more preoccupied with largely effortless pragmatic uses of media culture for the purposes of enhancing an international image and boosting the economy, the key term here being *branding*. International relations scholar Peter van Ham (2001, 3–4), for example, argues for the significance of the state's role in branding the nation in terms of international politics and the economy:

> Branding acquires its power because the right brand can surpass the actual products as a company's central asset. Smart firms pour most of their money into improving their brands, focusing more on the values and emotions that customers attach to them than on the quality of the products itself. . . . Smart states are building their brands around reputations and attitudes in the same way smart companies do.

Thus the state is strongly urged to play an active role in the production of attractive national cultural odor in the age of nation branding competition.[2]

In the course of the globalization of the idea of using media cultures as part of a national foreign policy strategy, the soft power argument has been replaced by a shallower policy discourse on the enhancement of international images. As a result, soft power is not so much being misunderstood and misappropriated as used to bolster a quite different logic at the level of cultural policy governing the national media culture. This is not to defend soft power discourse; Nye's soft power argument and nation branding share the basic principle of using media culture for the enhancement of a narrowly focused set of national interests, and attracting others and making others follow are both instances of unidirectional communication. However, a different, more pragmatic kind of manoeuver for the administration of culture has evolved. It legitimizes and relies on the marketization of culture and sponsors the inter-nationalized globalization of media culture. Its key concern is to promote the production and its international circulation of attractive media culture for the purpose of enhancing national images and economic profits in the international arena by way of branding the nation®.

The next chapter looks critically at the Japanese case, but we need to be cautious not to take nation branding policy discussion at its face value. What nation branding really means is ambiguous, and whether and how the nation can be branded is open to question from the marketing point of view (Fan 2010; Anholt 2013). The academic discussion of nation branding is not limited to the issues of marketing operations. To follow Ying Fan (2010, 101), nation branding can be more broadly defined in line with the discussion of soft power as "a process by which a nation's images can be created or altered, monitored, evaluated and proactively managed in order to enhance the country's reputation among a target international audience." Nation branding even in this sense is a messy, precarious business. There is no guarantee that the export of media culture enhances national images. Many actors within states, public relations advisory organizations, and media and cultural industries are involved in the project of nation branding with diverse intentions and approaches, which engender incoherent and contradictory policy actions (Aronczyk 2013). Also, it is rather difficult to judge whether and how nation brand images are enhanced. Only an elaborated ethnography of policy implementation and people's reception process would help us fully understand the complicated process of nation branding.

However, an issue relevant to this chapter is the discursive and performative power nation branding has to socially institute a national outlook. Recently, critical scholarly attention has been paid more to its relevance to the reconstruction of national identity (e.g., Jansen 2008; Volcic and Andrejevic 2011; Aronczyk 2013). The international projection of attractive images of a nation eventually necessitates the rearticulation of the selective narratives, symbolic meanings, and widely accepted stereotypical images of that nation to be appealingly represented as a coherent entity. The growing interest in nation branding drives the search for the distinctive cultural assets of the nation and the redemarcation of a "core" national culture. In explicating the global popularity of the animation and *otaku* culture of Japan, for example, it is often claimed that they inherited their national cultural essence from premodern Japan. The Edo culture of the eighteenth century is said to be the root of the contemporary Japanese cool cultures, and the necessity of reevaluating Japanese traditional cultural sensitivities and aesthetics is proposed in order to further promote Japanese media culture and enhance Japan's soft power (e.g., Okuno 2010). Furthermore, a growing interest in promoting South Korean and Japanese products in the world instigates racialized discourses of national culture and its ownership that confirm the nation's distinctive cultural aesthetics, styles, and tastes with the metaphor of a "cultural gene" or "cultural DNA."[3] As one policy maker of "Japan Brand project" states, what is necessary is to redefine "Japan" and to seriously consider how to properly discern Japanese cultural DNA and strategically standardize it so as to successfully input it into Japanese products and services.[4]

Such representation of national culture is eventually projected toward the national citizens (Varga 2014; Volcic and Andrejevic; Aronczyk 2013; Kaneva 2011). While the key aim of nation branding is considered to be the international projection of attractive images of the nation, it is not just externally oriented but also internally directed. As Sue Jansen (2008, 122) argues, "Branding not only explains nations to the world but also reinterprets national identity in market terms and provides new narratives for domestic consumption." This has been accompanied by the extension of the mutually constitutive relationship of the national/internal and the international/external. The construction of national identity is always closely related to international appraisal ("how they perceive us") as well as the representation of the foreign ("not like us"), against which the distinctiveness of the nation ("who we are") can be demarcated. Especially, the gaze of the significant other, most prevalently the Euro-American other, is constitutive of the discursive construction of national identity in non-Western countries such as Japan, where Western Orientalism and self-Orientalism function in a complicit manner (Iwabuchi 1994). The Euro-American gaze still occupies the dominant position. However, as nationality has come to be "constituted through specific local places, symbols and landscapes, icons of the nation central to that culture's location within the contours of global business, travel, branding" (Urry 2003, 87), wide-ranging and reciprocated international gazes have come to play a key role in the formation of national identity, whereby the idea and practice of nation branding rehighlights the nation-state as the most meaningful cultural entity of collective identification.

BANAL INTER-NATIONALISM

It can be argued that the representation of the nation in market terms is superficial and ahistorical, lacking the substantial depth and coherence of national narratives. Furthermore, as Nadia Kaneva (2011, 11) argues, while "branded imagination seeks to infiltrate and subsume the symbolic order of nationhood," there is no guarantee that it succeeds in internally obtaining people's consent over the national narrative with which they are encouraged to identify. Nevertheless, the action of searching for a legitimate content to be filled in the national form itself endorses a given existence of "authentic" national culture. As Mellisa Aronczyk (2013, 176) argues: "The mundane practices of nation branding do perpetuate the nation form. Why? Because they perpetuate a conversation about what the nation is *for* in a global context." This suggests that the practice of nation branding and people's participation in it work to confirm the nation as a form of collective identification and belonging. In this sense, it can be argued that nation branding plays a parallel role to the reconstruction of "imagined communities" (Anderson 1984) as it involves a call for people's participation in the mass ritual of nation branding as well as the renewed representation of the nation. Nation branding domestically generates the mobilization of citizens, who are encouraged to join in branding as "representatives, stakeholders and customers of the brand": "Citizens are called upon to 'live the brand' and hence to act and think in ways that are well suited to the general contours of the national brand" (Varga 2014, 836). People are thus invited to perform as ambassadors of the nation branding campaign.

Whether such an invitation is really embraced by people is highly questionable, but the coaction of the marketization of media cultures and associated policies of nation branding has broadly propagated, to say the least, an idea among the populace that the promotion of national branding via media culture must be taken seriously as it is of grave importance for national interests. Additionally, there is a more mundane and modest form of mass participation prevalent among the general public. We have observed a rapid development of global televised spectacles of various kinds in which people are asked to purchase a ticket to become part of the event and display a particular national symbol (Roche 2000). Moreover, with the amplification of actual or virtual participation in the number of international occasions, people are encouraged to confirm a sense of belonging to a particular nation. Such occasions provoke people to feel a sense of national pride when "our" national cultures do well. Or it might stir up a sense of regret, anger, and frustration when others beat "us." In Japan, the international standing of national culture has become even more of an important resource for the evocation of national pride due to the decline of the Japanese economy since the early 1990s. A 2010 survey on which aspects of Japan people are proud of showed that while Japan's technology and traditional culture were still conceived of as the most significant, 90 percent of respondents in their twenties and 80 percent of those in their thirties stated that they were proud of Japanese animation and computer games ("Poll: 95% Fear for Japan's Future" 2010). Not only does this reflect the fact that animation and computer games actually have been circulating well in the world but also reflects a widely shared perception that these items are key cultural commodities for the enhancement of Japan's soft power.

It can be argued that this merely displays a trivial, transient consumption of and identification with the idea of the nation, lacking substantial meanings of the narrative of the nation and, thus, of the expression of national pride. For example, in a presentation about the evocation of nationalist sentiment among young people in Japan participating in international cultural events and observing the ascent of Japanese culture in the world, Japanese university students stated, from their own experiences, that "Japanese nationalism is a fashion statement. It is something like owning a brand commodity. People do not care about the origin, history meaning and value of the ideas of 'Japan'" (Kwansai Gakuin 2006). John Fox (2006, 232) argues in his examination of the rise of nationalist sentiment through national holiday commemorations and international football competitions that the participation in such occasions elevates the sense of a national belonging, but this does not necessarily mean the rise of nationalistic sentiment: "While holidays and sports had the capacity to make the students national, there is little to suggest that they made them nationalist . . . any experience of collective belonging neither led to nor followed from heightened nationalist sensitivities." This is rather an important reminder that we should not jump to the conclusion of a rise of nationalism in the age of global interconnectedness without making a close analysis on people's participation in the international cultural event.[5]

Distinguishing between national cohesion and nationalist passion, Fox (2006, 232) further suggests that "national content does not follow unambiguously from national form." It can be argued, however, that the increase in the international cultural encounter that "makes people national" also needs to be taken seriously for the firm infiltration of a sense of national belonging and identification eventually takes a nonassertive, banal form. Michael Billig (1995) has argued that national feeling is facilitated and displayed by means of such mundane performances as casually showing the national flag in the city. The banal practice of national belonging is further promoted by an increase in encounters with people, goods, and images from many parts of the world and a plethora of international events and spectacles, which facilitate a mundane form of people "living the national brand." While this development might open up a possibility of cultivating new kinds of conception and imagination that goes beyond an exclusive framework of the nation, it more often than not engenders banal inter-nationalism as it prompts people to implicitly comprehend cross-cultural encounters as those among mutually exclusive national cultures with the delimited boundaries. With the entrenched permeation of an assumption that the global is the congregation of nations and that cultural diversity is comprehended mostly as that between nations, the conception of the nation as a (brand) form or a container based on territorial understanding of culture gains wider currency. Banal inter-nationalism has made methodological nationalism no longer just an academic matter but a part of people's mundane practice.

INTER-NATIONALIZED CULTURAL DIVERSITY AND MARGINALIZED CULTURAL DIFFERENCES

The cojoined operation of market-driven globalization and nation branding engenders banal inter-nationalism. Pervading the thinking and feeling that the nation is the unit of global cultural exchange, it reinforces the cardinal importance of the nation as a cultural form, which people identify with, belong to, and show loyalty to, and newly induces the sense of national belonging and the ownership of national culture. This might take an assertive shape of nationalistic clash over the ownership of culture. For example, the rise of "soft power competition" has given rise to and added fuel to the flames of the vicious circle of antagonistic nationalism in Asia. Recent Indonesian condemnation of a Malaysian tourism campaign in terms of the ownership of Bali dance culture and Chinese criticism of the distortion of historical representation in the South Korean drama series *Jumong 2* shows the increasing role that media culture plays in provoking disputes over the ownership of national culture and historical narrative in the inter-national arena.

Although not necessarily engendering xenophobic aggression, banal inter-nationalism implicitly and explicitly engenders exclusionary politics of the nation, as it newly provokes the clear demarcation of "us" and "them" through an inter-national administration of cultural diversity. This is to take seriously Richard Wilk's (1995, 118) argument that the hegemony of the global cultural system is "not of content, but of form." While globalization organizes cultural diversity through form, it is not inclusive of various kinds of social and cultural differences. The instituting of globally shared container forms and cultural formats generate a certain mode of cultural diversity, and this indicates the operation of cultural hegemony that "celebrate(s) particular kinds of diversity while submerging, deflating or suppressing others" (1995, 118). Banal inter-nationalism highlights a nation-based cultural diversity of the world, not attending to marginalized differences and multicultural situations within the nation.

While nation branding renders the narration of the nation highly commercialized, dehistoricized, and incoherent, such narratives are still based on an essentialist conception of the nation as an organic cultural entity and do not pay due attention to the diversity within the nation-state (Kaneva 2011). While nation branding from time to time supports minority groups' traditional culture or promotes tokenized multicultural commodities in an international arena, the kinds of media culture promoted for international circulation are chiefly those that are commercially mainstream in their countries of origin, and there is not much space for socially and culturally marginalized voices within the nation. Such exercise of nation branding fails to bear in mind that national borders are discursively drawn in such a way as to suppress various sociocultural differences within and disavow their existence as constitutive of the nation.

As is discussed in the following chapters, the suppression of cultural diversity within the national borders might take the form of candid suppression by the nation branding policy and the straightforward application of banal inter-nationalism to the media representation of the multicultural situation. Or the progression of inter-nationalized media cultural flows and connections further sidelines the recognition of hyphenated subjects such as Asian/Japanese Americans living in the United States or resident Koreans in Japan. This issue of the inter-nationalized promotion of cultural diversity deterring the due appreciation of cultural diversity within national borders is never new. It is reminiscent of a crucial point raised by Edward Said's seminal work, *Orientalism* (1978), about how the dichotomized construction of culturally coherent entities exerts symbolic violence onto the lively reality of a human society full of cultural diversity. While Western Orientalism has been countered by oriental Occidentalism or self-Orientalism, it is often argued, the two discourses are not in conflict but in collusion in that they mutually, though unevenly, construct culturally coherent entities in separation (Iwabuchi 1994). The covert victim of an interaction of Orientalism and self-Orientalism thus are those who are excluded, marginalized, and silenced in each society as their presence and experience of marginalization are further disregarded.

The operation of intercultural marginalization of this kind also takes more subtle forms with the intensification of cross-border mobility of media culture and people. One complicated case is the impact of inter-nationalized cultural exchange on the social recognition and (dis)empowerment of migrants and diasporas. The key problem here is the oversimplified identification of migrants and diasporas with their home countries. Critical researchers of Asian Australian studies stated the following regarding the enduring stereotypical images of Chinese migrants and diasporas in Australia: "As we become more dependent on the dollars from the economies of Asia, I would hope that the vestige of 19th century orientalism will fade away" (Kwok et al. 2004). This statement refers to an expectation of a positive impact of the rise of their "home" countries' economy and culture on the social appreciation of migrants and diasporas. The sense of "hope" expressed above is well taken, and it might be the case that the rise of Chinese economy would not just improve international images of China but also enhance social recognition of those diasporas/migrants who identify themselves and are identified as "Chinese" in the host society.

However, there is no guarantee that this is the case. Even if the rise of Asian economy and culture might make a classical mode of Orientalism less relevant, geopolitically driven cultural Othering dies hard. It is well known that the rise of Japanese economy in the 1970s and 1980s reproduced Orientalist images such as "economic animal" or "techno-Orientalism" (Iwabuchi 1994). Likewise, the rise of Chinese economy actually induces negative reactions in other countries, and this might even lead to a harmful effect on people of Chinese descent living abroad. A negative effect on migrants and diasporas in the host country can also be exerted by the conspicuous rise of the home country's culture. Furthermore, even if the rise of the host country's media culture has an empowering impact on hyphenated subjects via the improvement of the images of that nation, this does not guarantee facilitation of the full recognition of marginalized subjects as members of the host society. It might further strengthen the perception of their "national" affiliation as other than "ours," hence reinforcing the multicultural containment of "their" difference. There is a thin line between the empowerment of diasporas by their association with the images of the home country and the confusion of their identities and differences with those living in the home country, as will be discussed in chapter 5 in terms of how the popularity of South Korean media cultures has impinged on the social recognition of resident Koreans.

A crucial point here is an assumption that migrants and diasporas are self-evidently identical with and representative of the nation-state of their descent. And it is this apparent axiom that should be seriously questioned. The sympathetic reception of media culture improves the images of the nation-state that exports it, which might lead to enhancing the social recognition of diasporas/migrants of that country's descent in the host society. However, whether its impact is positive or negative, the presumed identification of hyphenated subjects with their home countries is problematic since it tends to be co-opted by banal inter-nationalism and discourages serious appreciation of cultural diversity and full engagement with multicultural questions within the nation. Banal inter-nationalism precludes a nuanced understanding of the diasporic negotiation of "where one is from" and "where one is at" (Ang 2001) by refusing to acknowledge that she or he is a member of "our" society here.

RELENTLESS SUSPICION OF
THE EXCLUSIONARY FORCE

While the impossibility of the modern project of constructing a culturally coherent nation has been made even more apparent as sociocultural diversity within the nation has been further intensifying due to transborder ethnocultural flows, this does not mean the displacing of mutually exclusive boundaries of imagined communities. We have been witnessing the demise of multiculturalism together with tightening the measures of border control. In tandem with this, the inter-national administration of cultural diversity through the promotion of cultural export and exchange with "foreign" cultures has evolved. Crossing national cultural borders is much encouraged, but chiefly in a nontransgressive manner that mundanely strengthens the clear demarcation of national borders and renders their exclusionary politics inconsequential.

To go beyond a banal inter-nationalism that fortifies national outlook, theoretical transcendence of methodological nationalism is not enough. Beck's (2006) argument of "banal cosmopolitanism" is suggestive in this regard. Its main purpose is to engage with the possibility of advancing cosmopolitanism in society. This is not to negate the continuing significance of the territorially delimited nation-state in our analysis but puts forward the necessity of differently reimagining and ameliorating it from a cosmopolitan perspective. Moreover, much effort is needed to make such imagination and outlook, which displaces and transcends banal inter-nationalism, widely instituted in society. In relation to this, let us be reminded of another classical insight of a crucial point of Said's *Orientalism*, which is, as James Clifford (1988, 273) points out, a "relentless suspicion of totality" about any notions of distinct human groups, cultures, and geographical spaces. It seems rather imperative for researchers to strive to make such relentless suspicion part of mundane social praxis if we are to undo the resilience of exclusive national cultural boundaries. I return to the issue in the final chapter, but the close examination of several ways in which inter-nationalized circulation, promotion, and consumption of media culture subtly override the issue of cultural diversity and multicultural questions within the nation in the Japanese context should come first.

NOTES

1. Beck's argument is criticized for being too ruthless to prominent sociological works. For an extensive critique from a sociological perspective, see Kendall, Woodward, and Skribs (2009, 54–75).

2. For more on "cultural odor," see Iwabuchi (2002a).

3. For the South Korean case, see Cho (2011); for the Japanese case, see, for example, www.kanto.meti.go.jp/seisaku/uec.../lec01_kouen_22fy.pdf.

4. For example, blogs.yahoo.co.jp/hiromi_ito2002jp/57705983.html and www.kanto.meti. go.jp/seisaku/uec.../lec01_kouen_22fy.pdf.

5. This is reminiscent of the case of FIFA Soccer World Cup in 2002, cohosted by South Korea and Japan. Some observed the rise of "petit-nationalism" in Japan (Kayama 2002) as a massive number of ordinary Japanese—especially young people—cheerfully and innocently rejoiced at being Japanese together in a public space: they waved the national flag, painted it on their faces, and sang the national anthem in praise of the emperor's everlasting rule. These kinds of conduct had long tended to be restrained in the public space as they were considered a

negative reminder of Japanese imperialism. Such practices attracted much discussion in Japan as some thought it a potentially dangerous expression that could easily lead to an exclusive cultural nationalism. However, this phenomenon should not be interpreted as the rise of a fanatical nationalism since the survey regularly shows that only a small portion of Japanese youths feel a substantial sense of pride in their country. For example, in a public opinion survey, only 15 percent of respondents feel that way. See *Asahi Shinbun*, March 16, 2005.

Chapter Two

Cool Japan, Brand Nationalism, and the Public Interest

As culture as a form of meaning construction and a process of communication is ubiquitous in all social activities—which necessarily are power laden—culture extends its relevance and strategic usefulness to spheres beyond itself. As George Yúdice (2003) argues, culture has become an expedient "resource" that allows various social actors to pursue their own political, economic, communal, and activist interests. Various social actors, including marginalized persons and nongovernmental organizations (NGOs), have engaged in identity politics and become involved in new social movements by resorting to the expediency of culture. That said, the media and culture industries have especially been attuned to the instrumental value of culture, having used it most effectively and aggressively for commercial purposes. At the same time, as shown by the prevalence of soft power and nation branding in the discussion of cultural policy, states have also shown a strong interest in developing media cultures together with other service sectors, which have come to play a significant role in the national and global economy. Japan is no exception. The growing international attention to media culture as a useful resource for the projection of appealing images of the nation has pressed the development of a highly pragmatic and opportunistic cultural policy in Japan. While the national policy of using culture in the pursuit of national interests is not new in Japan, the recent development signifies a new collaborative relationship among the state and media and cultural industries and between culture and national interest.

This chapter looks at how the uses of media culture for national interests have been discussed in the Japanese context by critically examining the recent development of cultural policy arguments that aim to internationally heighten Japan's brand image and the expansion of cultural export that accompanies it. While soft power is the most common cultural policy concept in Japan, "Cool Japan" has become a corresponding umbrella catchphrase that integrates both political (i.e., cultural/public diplomacy) and economic (i.e., creative industries) objectives of cultural policy. I argue that the stemming institutionalization of opportunistic cultural policy concerns functions as "brand nationalism," whose narrowly focused national interest implicitly and explicitly discourages engagement with crucial cultural issues that are raised by the market-driven, conflict-laden, and re-nationalizing process of globalization. The development of cultural policy of this kind significantly thwarts the advancement of media culture's capacity to enhance cross-border dialogue and promote hitherto marginalized voices and cultural expressions in the public sphere.

RISE OF THE "COOL JAPAN" POLICY

Since the early 1990s when the so-called post-bubble economy collapsed, Japan has been struggling with economic downturn. Its prolonged dire situation was further highlighted by the rise of other Asian economies, such as China and India, in the new millennium. Instead, what attracted wider attention in the same period is the rise of Japanese media culture in the world (i.e., specifically including Europe and the United States). We have witnessed, at least since the early 1990s, the emergence of "soft" nationalism in Japan— that is, a narcissist discourse on the global spread of Japanese popular cultural "software," such as Japanese animation and video games, set against technological "hardware" (Iwabuchi 2002b). But the scale and extent of euphoria is much larger in early twenty-first-century Japan. In their 2003 album titled *MIJ*, for example, the then most popular idol group in Japan, SMAP declares a sense of pride in observing the spread of Japanese cultures and Japanese people whose cultural works are renowned in the world:

> There has been no time when so many Japanese are in the world centre stages. While Japan is not economically vigorous, now is a great historical moment to Japan. Isn't it really good for us to live as Japanese at this moment? News coverage on those Japanese who are doing fascinating works in the world makes us empowered and feel proud to be Japanese. . . . Our slogan is MIJ = Made in Japan!

The international advent of Japanese media culture was in sharp contrast to the fall of the Japanese economy and thus inspired a social and personal lift in a stagnated Japan.

There is actually some ground for this self-praise. The spread of Japanese media culture such as animation, comic books, cute icons like Hello Kitty, video games, and cosplay performance into the United States and Europe has been a gradual and steady phenomenon since at least the 1980s, but it has much expanded in the new millennium, so much so that we have recently witnessed the emergence of a "Cool Japan" discourse, which discusses the global spread of Japanese media and consumer cultures in a celebratory manner. It is the attention devoted to this phenomenon by the Euro-American media that has given credence to the advent of a "Cool Japan." Several commentators have attested to Japan's growing cultural influence in the last several years: "During the 1990s, Japan became associated with its economic stagnation. However, what many failed to realize is that Japan has transformed itself into a vibrant culture-exporting country during the 1990s" (cited in Koshikawa 2003); "Japan's influence on pop culture and consumer trend runs deep" (Palmeri and Byrnes 2004); "Japan is reinventing itself on earth—this time as the coolest nation culture" (Faiola 2003). Coining the term *gross national cool* (GNC), an American journalist even announced the rise of Japan as a cultural superpower in the international arena (McGray 2002). This journalistic article was quickly translated into Japanese and widely referred to as evidence of the rise of Japanese cultural power in the world. However, it should be noted that despite the fact that Japanese media culture has been much more actively and massively received in Asian countries, this has never spurred the same extent of euphoria. As was the case with traditional cultures such as Ukiyoe, Western appreciation still has a determining power on the international quality of Japanese culture. Cool Japan discourse still in this sense testifies to Japan's appreciation of the Western Orientalist gaze in the assessment of Japan's cultural status and Japan's complicit uses of it to enhance a sense of national pride both domestically and internationally (Iwabuchi 1994). In this sense, it can be argued that Cool Japan is basically a Western phenomenon.

The Euro-American endorsement of the spread of Japanese media culture has further cheered up people in Japan; however, the Japanese embracing of Cool Japan marks a crucial difference in two respects. One is the discernment of "Japanese-ness." In the 1990s, when soft nationalism discourse was prevalent, there was a deep-seated difficulty in observing the global spread of Japanese cultural product and clearly discerning whether and how Japanese cultural products are "Japanese," both in their representation and in the dynamic process of transcultural consumption: the universal appeal of Japanese cultural products seemed to accompany the disappearance of any perceptible "Japaneseness" (see Iwabuchi 2002b). However, this difficulty seems to have disappeared in the twenty-first century. Although the question of whether and how Japanese media culture such as animations and characters invoke the image of Japanese culture and lifestyle is still a moot one, what is indisputable is that a large number of young people in the United States and Europe, as well as Asia, has come to regard Japan as a creative country capable of producing attractive characters, imaginaries, and commodities.

This shift in the perception of Japanese "cultural odor" has been induced by the advancement of a dynamic process of decentering and recentering, in which the transnational alliance of media and cultural industries strategically encourages the marketing of more non-Western media contents in the world markets.

More importantly, the Japanese embracing of Cool Japan distinguishes itself from the previous discourse in that it is not just limited to a celebratory nationalistic euphoria but has accompanied the active development of national cultural policy discussion and implementation aimed at further enhancing Japan's cultural standing in the world. As discussed in the previous chapter, this shift has been pushed under the growing policy concern in the world with the enhancement of national interests in terms of both economy and foreign policy through nation branding. The key policy term for this purpose in Japan is soft power. When he first advocated "soft power" in the early 1990s, Joseph Nye dismissed Japan's soft power as negligible. His contention was that Japan was a "one-dimensional economic power," with its consumer commodities—no matter how globally spread—still lacking an associated "appeal to a broader set of values" (Nye 1990, 32). However, more than ten years later, when "soft power" regained currency in the context of the Bush administration's hard-liner policies, Nye (2005) has come to acknowledge Japan's cultural influence in the world: "Japan's popular culture was still producing potential soft-power resources even after its economy slowed down. Now, with signs of a reviving economy, Japan's soft power may increase even more."

This was another welcome endorsement of Japan's soft power by a U.S. authority. Nye was often invited by the Japanese government, think-tanks, and mass media to confirm the rising soft power of Japan to the Japanese populace through lectures, translated publications, and media interviews. The Japanese government also officially began to announce its policy orientation toward the enhancement of soft power publicly. For example, the 2003 Japanese Cultural Agency's gathering for discussion about international cultural exchange states:

> In the twenty-first century, "soft power," which is the capacity to attract foreign nations by the appeal of lifestyle and culture of the nation, is more important than military power. Japan as the nation rich in attractive cultures is expected to make an international contribution through international cultural exchange and actively display the 21st century model of soft power. [1]

The Japanese government has become much interested in the development of "content" industries (which have been replaced by "creative industries" since 2010 as mentioned below) as well as in the promotion of cultural diplomacy, both of which are supposed to be facilitated by the enhancement of the international images of Japan through media cultures. Since the turn of the century, many committees focusing on the promotion of Japanese media culture have been established by the government and by think-tanks, especially under the Koizumi government (2001–2006), including the Head Office for Intellectual Property Strategy (2002), the Committee for Tourism Nation (2003), the Committee for Info-Communication Software (2003), the Research Committee for Content Business (2005), the J-Brand Initiative (2003), the e-Japan Strategy (2003), and the Council for the Promotion of International Exchange (on the Strengthening of Cultural Dispatch) (2006). The Ministry of Foreign Affairs (MOFA) also became active in incorporating the uses of media culture for the advancement of cultural diplomacy. MOFA integrated two distinct ministry sections devoted, respectively, to cultural diplomacy and international cultural exchange and international publicity into a single Public Diplomacy Department in 2004. Public diplomacy was also for the first time officially taken up in the *2004 Diplomatic Bluebook*, and in 2006, MOFA officially adopted "pop-culture diplomacy" as "its primary tools for cultural diplomacy."[2] Aiming to boost Japan's brand image through the international projection of Japanese media culture, the ministry appointed popular animation character Doraemon as anime ambassador in 2008 and three young, female fashion leaders as ambassadors of cute. These ambassadors are assigned to travel the world to promote Japanese culture abroad. MOFA also supports the World Cosplay Summit, which has been held annually in Japan.

At the same time, the term *Cool Japan* had gradually gained currency as an umbrella term to cover all areas of interests in nation branding, especially after the publication of the GNC article.[3] Finally, the Ministry of Economy, Trade and Industry (METI) established the Cool Japan promotion office in June 2010. The cabinet secretariat set up "the Council for the Promotion of Cool Japan" in 2013, and 50 billion yen has been included in the national budget in 2013 for setting up infrastructures to promote Japanese contents overseas for the purpose of letting the charm of Japanese culture (not just media contents but various cultures such as food, fashion, traditional craft, and Japanese ways of life) be widely spread and embraced in the world. This development suggests an emerging trend that a policy concern with the economic benefit of exporting media culture under the name of creative industries is growing. METI actually adopted the term *creative industries* for the English translation of the Cool Japan promotion office. The facilitation of nation branding and Cool Japan is also included in MOFA's public diplomacy policy, while MOFA emphasizes that the enhancement of Japan's cultural standing in the world should precede even in such policy discussions on the grounds that the purpose of the promotion of Japanese media culture should not be reduced to market profits only.[4] There is still no single ministry that plans and implements a coherent cultural policy, but the significance of utilizing media cultures to enhance Japan's soft power and nation branding has been widely and cooperatively discussed by various ministries and government offices in Japan, and associated policy practices have been implemented under the name of Cool Japan in the new millennium.

BRAND NATIONALISM AND ITS
IDEOLOGICAL CLOSURE

Like all nation branding policies, the effectiveness of the Cool Japan policy in selling more Japanese cultural products and enhancing certain national images, as policymakers contend, is dubious. Careful research on how Japanese media culture is marketed and consumed in the world would reveal the intricate ways of international cultural flows, which do not easily meet the expectations of those who advocate Cool Japan and nation branding. And only comprehensive research that attends to the complexity of uneven cultural globalization in terms of production, representation, and consumption would tell us about the actualized effect of such a policy. Nevertheless, its impact is nontrivial inasmuch as it accompanies the material institutionalization and fiscal funding and, more crucially, advances a pragmatic understanding of the usefulness of culture and the role of cultural policy. The issue at stake is not limited to whether or not the Cool Japan policy is well designed and implemented to sell more Japanese cultural products and branded images. An even more significant question is whether and how the series of cultural policy discussions is concerned with tackling the imperative cultural issues that cultural globalization processes have underscored.

I would argue that this is not the case with the cultural policy discussion in Japan, for it is opportunistic, self-contradictory, and suppressive. It is opportunistic because the main discussion is how to make the best use of existing international appeal (supposed as such) of Japanese media culture as an export commodity without tackling the improvement of working environments to enhance creativity and globally structured issues such as labor conditions and copyright control. It is self-contradictory since, while emphasizing the significance of soft power policy for the advancement of international exchange and dialogue, the Japanese government eventually has dealt with historical and territorial issues in East Asia in a way that is obviously detrimental to the enhancement of soft power and the advancement of international dialogue. And Japan's cultural policy discussion is suppressive because it does not care about and even ignores crucial policy questions concerning who are the beneficiaries of cultural policy and whose culture, interest, and voice are attended to. This point is related to the gap between the promotion of Cool Japan and engagement with intensifying multicultural situations in Japan, as well as how the former has been pursued at the cost of the latter. In sum, what matters is not so much the effectiveness of Japan's cultural policy as its ideological closure, which can be called *brand nationalism*. Japan's pursuit of narrowly focused national interests contains the discussion of what cultural policy should engage in the service of wider public interests.

The policy discussion of Cool Japan is clearly founded on an assumption that Japan's cultural products have already attained international attractiveness and that the main concern is how to further promote them by creating new platforms, distribution networks, and exhibition events. The key policy strategy of creative industries is thus opportunistic as it focuses on support for the international expansion of supposedly already lucrative content/creative industries rather than planning a comprehensive policy for developing content/creative industries. Actually, Japanese media and cultural industries and many creators are skeptical of the effectiveness of the state's policy to help new kinds of cultural creativity originating in Japan flourish and whether the advancement of the export of media cultural products would be of any benefit to creators in Japan.[5] This does not mean, however, that media and cultural industries do not need any support from the state. The affluent domestic market has not encouraged most Japanese media and cultural industries to develop export-oriented business models. The total export amount of Japanese media culture is around just 5 percent of domestic market revenue. As the increasing international competition and the saturation of domestic markets are pushing media and cultural industries to enter the international market, a policy to facilitate export would be helpful to them. However, even more imperative for the industries and creators is the improvement of the domestic working environment to allow creators to enhance productive competence in order to win the international rivalry in terms of the training of creators, the improvement of labor conditions, and the settlement of copyright issues for their advantage. But these matters have not yet been seriously considered in the Cool Japan policy discussion.

In 2006, then foreign minister Taro Aso delivered a speech to would-be creators who were learning creative skills related to the production of digital cultures at a creator training school, Digital Hollywood, near Akihabara. Aso praised the creativity of Japanese animation and manga, which had significantly elevated Japan's brand image, and asked for the students' help for and active participation in further enhancing the "Japan brand" to successfully push forward public diplomacy. Yet a very crucial issue did not concern him at all, which was the improvement of the actual working conditions of animation subcontractors. Those conditions are infamously poor, and there is no sign of improvement. Many young creators are forced to leave the industries due to low wages. According to *Yomiuri* newspaper (March 20, 2013), the average annual income for workers in their twenties is just 1.1 million yen, 2.14 million yen for those in their thirties, and 4.01 million yen for those in their forties. All figures are far below the national average, and the income for workers in their twenties is one-third of the national average. Given that a large amount of money is slated to be invested for the Cool Japan project, many creators are suspicious that the Cool Japan policy would only benefit the top circle of media and cultural industries in Japan.[6]

The exploitation of labor in media and cultural industries is not a domestic issue but a transnationally structured one. It needs to be reiterated that Japan's soft power turn and the advancement of the Cool Japan policy are part of the global trend of a growing concern with nation branding policy, which legitimizes and is facilitated by the penetration of market-driven globalization. This point is related to a vital limitation of Nye's argument about soft power. While Nye clearly distinguishes between culture as soft power and economy as hard power, a clear separation of economy and culture is untenable if we are to understand the power structure of market-driven globalization, as recent discussions of creative industries and content business would suggest. Capital has no loyalty to national borders but fosters the national market as the local unit while also requiring state regulation and control in order to make profits. States, for their part, are complicit in this process, for they work with it rather than regulating and controlling it for the public good. Likewise, while the development of creativity in the production of internationally appealing culture is emphasized, the Cool Japan policy does not give due attention to the issues of how media cultural production actually operates in the international political economy in which transnational media and cultural industries dominate the production process and the distribution channel.[7]

The high concentration of ownership in a handful of global media conglomerates and transnationally generating the horizontal and vertical integration they advance have accompanied the new international division of cultural labor (Miller et. al. 2005). While the headquarters of media and cultural industries are located in the global cities of wealthier countries, the production process is much decentered as the corporations are desperately seeking cheap labor by outsourcing basic works. This is not just occurring in Hollywood but also in cultural production within East Asia. For example, Japanese animation companies have long subcontracted the basic work of animation production to other parts of Asia. This work used to be sent to South Korea and Taiwan, but as labor costs have increased there, it is gradually shifting to other, cheaper locations, such as China. Those workers work hard with long labor hours for low wages, and the situation is even getting worse with the advancement of media globalization (see Yoon 2009).[8]

For global media conglomerates, copyright and intellectual property are the most important sources of profit for media and cultural industries, as is the case with the brand-manufacturing sector (Klein 2000). David Hesmondhalgh (2008) proposes to examine the copyright monopoly by media and cultural industries as the neoliberalism operation of cultural imperialism. He argues that the marketization of media culture has strengthened the view of culture as property, and the idea of creativity is shifting from a "social and collective" one to individualization, which is subtly exploited by transnational media and cultural industries on a global scale. As Eiji Otsuka and Nobuaki Osawa (2005) point out regarding the Japanese animation industries, without fundamentally changing the existing structure of profit-taking through the monopoly of distribution networks and copyrights by global media and cultural industries, the issue of uneven profit distribution will not be substantially improved. As global media conglomerates' oligopolistic control over copyrights has become a significant part of global cultural domination, whether and how the profits and benefits of the development of media and cultural industries actually return to media factory workers, both domestically and internationally, is an imperative matter for public discussion. Otherwise, national cultural policy would continue to lend itself to strengthening the global media conglomerate.

These issues of domestic and global unevenness and cultural domination by transnational media and cultural industries are what the national government should seriously tackle, given that there is no effective international political institution to take up the tasks. What we see instead, however, is a government that is highly motivated to promote national culture through collaboration with private corporations without engaging with transnationally structured issues of cultural economy.

DISCOURAGEMENT OF EAST ASIAN DIALOGUE

The globalization of soft power in tandem with the exercise of nation branding has, as discussed in the previous chapter, accompanied the unambiguous interest in enhancing nation's brand images through the promotion of media cultures, whereby the other significant cultural resources of soft power—respectful foreign policy and attractive democratic values established in the relevant society—have become redundant. In Japan, this line of nation branding policy was strongly advocated by a former Japanese foreign minister, Aso (who became prime minister in 2008). Aso's above-mentioned 2006 speech, delivered at Digital Hollywood, included the following statement regarding the significance of media culture for the policy of public/cultural diplomacy:

> We want pop culture, which is so effective in penetrating throughout the general public, to be our ally in diplomacy . . . one part of diplomacy lies in having a competitive brand image, so to speak. Now more than ever, it is impossible for this to stay entirely within the realm of the work of diplomats . . . what we need to do now is to build on this foundation [the fact that Japan already has achieved a good image] and attract people of the world to

Japanese culture, whether modern or that handed down from antiquity. (Aso 2006)

The flippancy of this kind of cultural diplomacy through nation branding was clearly revealed in its failure to form any sincere commitment to engage with lingering territorial issues and unresolved historical issues of Japanese colonialism and imperialism in other East Asian countries, especially in China and South Korea.

Referring to the 2006 BBC survey of national images, Aso then boasted about Japan being among the most favorably perceived nations in the world and proposed to promote nation's brand power further by exporting more attractive Japanese media cultures (especially manga and anime). However, he completely neglected the fact that in the survey two countries— China and South Korea—showed quite negative responses to the images of Japan. While the Koizumi government tried to promote cultural diplomacy policy quite aggressively, it actually escalated anti-Japanese sentiments in China and South Korea over the issues raised by history textbooks, long-standing territorial disputes, and Prime Minister Koizumi's relentless official visits to the Yasukuni Shrine. Actually, Nye points out that unresolved historical issues with other Asian countries are one of the crucial weaknesses of Japanese soft power, besides the lack of a migration policy (in spite of Japan's ageing population) and the cultural-linguistic particularism that indicates the extent to which Japan's cultural orientation is very much inward-looking (Nye 2005a). Nye publicly criticized Koizumi's repeated visits to the Yasukuni Shrine on account of its negative impact on Japan's soft power (Nye 2005b). While the Koizumi government emphasized the importance of widely disseminating Japanese media cultures for the purposes of establishing harmonious relations with other countries, it actually seriously damaged relations with neighboring countries by closing down dialogue.

Furthermore, the idea of cultural diplomacy tends to rely on a naïve assumption about media culture's capacity to improve Japan's reputation abroad and to transcend the problematic and historically constituted relations between Japan and other East and Southeast Asian countries. While the uses of culture and media communication to enhance Japan's image in the international arena began as early as the 1920s and 1930s, when Japan aspired to become an imperial and colonial power equivalent to Euro-American counterparts (Sato 2012), the cultural diplomacy policy of the postwar era was institutionalized in the 1970s as part of the so-called Fukuda Doctrine. The possibility of improving Japanese images in the region through the introduction of various Japanese cultures attracted serious attention from the state as anti-Japanese sentiments were aroused in Southeast Asian countries due to economic exploitation. While traditional cultures such as the tea ceremony and *kabuki* have been the main objects of cultural exchange, media cultures also attracted much attention in the late 1980s, when the popularity of TV drama series—especially *Oshin*, which became a phenomenal hit in many countries—noticeably testified to the capacity of media culture to enhance the international understanding of the "liberated" and "humane" faces of postwar Japan. The thought was that these media cultures could help over-come disapproving historical memories of Japanese colonialism and the neg-ative image of the country's economic exploitation of the region (see Iwabu-chi 2001).

The significance of disseminating Japanese media cultures was even more urgently discussed with the intensification of anti-Japanese demonstrations in China and South Korea in the early twenty-first century. There was still an effortless expectation that the spread of Japanese media culture would efface lingering antagonistic sentiments regarding Japan's history of imperialism and colonialism. When Aso was appointed foreign minister in 2005, he alleg-edly stated that Japan's relationship with China should be unproblematic inasmuch as many young people in China were reading Japanese manga. Here it is assumed that young people in China who like to consume Japanese media culture will feel more tolerant toward Japan and that increased exports of media culture to Asian markets thus automatically serve Japan's cultural diplomacy by smoothing out anti-Japanese sentiments in East Asia. Howev-er, the reality is far more complicated than such reasoning suggests. In South Korea and China, many of those who are happy to consume Japanese media culture actually consider historical issues separately and critically (Iwabuchi 2007). The coexistence of thoughts such as "I love Japanese comics" and "I cannot forget what Japan did to our grandparents" within the same person's mind is by no means ruled out. Even if a favorable consumption of Japanese media cultures might positively change the images of contemporary Japan, it neither erases the past nor people's memories of it. Historical issues need to be dealt with continuously and on their own terms.

Significantly missing in the discussion of the progression of cultural di-plomacy through the export of media cultures is what images and ideas of "Japan" are to be promoted, how their reception is complicated by the nature of various audiences, and how the circulation of media culture is to be locat-ed in a comprehensive cultural policy whose aims include not just the better-ment of the nation's brand images but the advancement of cross-border di-alogues among citizens. The discourse of cultural diplomacy, as shown above, does not aim to promote but rather thwarts a sincere engagement with "historical truthfulness," which can only be fostered through cross-border dialogues involving various citizens' views of the past (Morris-Suzuki 2005). To be sure, as I discuss in chapters 5 and 6, media cultural flows in East Asia have facilitated mutual understandings in an unprecedented manner. Expo-sure to the media culture of Japan would more or less enhance the under-standing of culture and society in Japan, even if in a one-way manner. However, extra efforts would be needed to direct the international promotion of Japanese media culture into pathways of mutuality and exchange. What cultural policy needs to carefully consider is whether and how we can develop East Asian media and cultural connections into a good opportunity for furthering citizens' possibly conflict-laden dialogues without assuming that media culture has the magical power to overcome historical issues.

With the growing currency of the METI-driven Cool Japan policy, MOFA also officially announced its support of the policy, emphasizing its diplomatic significance that goes beyond economic interests. While "pop-culture diplomacy" is still one of the main policy actions of cultural exchange, however, MOFA puts more emphasis on public diplomacy as opposed to cultural diplomacy and restructured cultural diplomacy sections by establishing the Public Diplomacy Strategy Division in 2012, which integrates the three sections of press release, publicity, and cultural exchange. Public diplomacy does not just aim to improve soft power via nation branding but, more importantly, strives to effectively publicize Japan's opinions and standpoints about diplomatic matters to the world and enhance Japan's international presence.[9] This shift is suggestive of Japan's changing relationship with China and South Korea. The rise of soft power in the two countries in terms of the export of media culture, overseas language education, and tourism accompanies the relative decline of Japan's presence in the international community. Even more crucial is Japan's lingering historical and territorial disputes with the two countries, which have been worsened since the inauguration of the Abe cabinet in 2012. China and South Korea have become not so much the main target countries of pop-culture diplomacy as tough rivals in the competition of soft power and public diplomacy, and this shift shows even less prospect of policy intervention to promote cross-border dialogue.

UN-ENGAGING WITH CULTURAL
DIVERSITY WITHIN JAPAN

Recently, the scope of cultural diplomacy has been expanded to place greater emphasis on the fostering of mutuality and cultural exchange (Holden 2013). Likewise, it is claimed in a Japanese policy statement of cultural diplomacy that the advancement of international cultural exchange, rather than the use of hard military power, will be key to the creation of a peaceful world where cultural diversity is mutually respected and celebrated and multilateral understanding and dialogue is promoted ("Bunka gaiko" 2005). Although mutuality is much stressed, what the policy eventually aims to promote is a one-way projection of the appealing images of a nation and the promotion of a nation-based kind of intercultural dialogue and cultural diversity while hindering internal cultural diversity. In addition to the absence of sincere commitment to the advancement of cross-border dialogue over historical issues in East Asia, Japanese cultural policy's preoccupation with the projection and enhancement of the nation's brand images in the world has a serious drawback when it comes to any engagement with sociocultural democratization of the kind that does justice to hitherto marginalized voices and diversity in society.

This is shown not just by the market-oriented aspiration for nation branding facilitating the reessentialization of the ownership of a "core" national culture in an exclusive manner, as discussed in chapter 1. More significantly, it makes the question of who is excluded and whose voices are suppressed in society irrelevant and further hinders paying due attention to postcolonial and multicultural issues within Japan. One explicit example of how nation branding suppresses the policy concern with cultural diversity within Japan is the development of NHK World. In early 2006, the expansion of international broadcasting services had begun to be seriously discussed in Japan, and the services commenced in February 2009 with the purpose of enhancing Japan's national image in the world for the promotion of political and economic interests. However, discussion of the service first started when foreign nationals residing in Japan complained to then prime minister Koizumi about Japan's lack of broadcasting in languages other than Japanese. So, what was at stake in the beginning was the failure of the Japanese broadcasting system to provide due public service to people of diverse ethnic and linguistic backgrounds who were residing in Japan. The question of the broadcasting system's publicness, in the sense of doing justice to the diversity of citizens whose voices and concerns are not well reflected in the mass media, is indeed an urgent one inasmuch as Japanese society is becoming more multicultural. In connection with my own research, I have often heard similar complaints from foreign nationals residing in Japan. However, in the cabinet meeting a few days later, these concerns were translated into a strategy aimed at the enhancement of national images and conveying the opinions of the Japanese government to the world by developing an English-language international broadcasting service. The nation branding policy clearly suppresses a vital cultural policy engagement with the task of bringing the hitherto marginalized voices and concerns of various citizens into the public sphere and of ensuring that those voices are heard.

This is also a reminder of the striking gap between the rapid progression of cultural policy to promote the international circulation of Japanese media culture and the under-development of multicultural policy. Japan has long been a multicultural and multiethnic nation. No small number of racial and ethnic minorities inhabits Japan's multicultural spectrum, such as resident Koreans and Chinese, indigenous Ainu people, as well as the people of marginalized regions like Okinawa. Since the late 1980s, attracted by the strong Japanese economy and yen, many people from Asia and Latin America (mostly Japanese Brazilians and Japanese Peruvians, descendants of those who emigrated in the early twentieth century) as well as other parts of the world entered Japan as workers and marriage migrants. According to data from the Ministry of Justice's website, the number of foreign nationals living in Japan was about 2.07 million at the end of 2013, while it was 1.22 million in 1991.[10] If we include those who have Japanese nationality, the number of ethnic minorities are much larger. Japanese policymakers have belatedly begun discussing the growing multicultural situation. In 2005, the Committee for the Promotion of Multicultural Co-living (*tabunka kyousei*) was established by the Ministry of Internal Affairs and Communications of Japan, and in the subsequent year, its report "Towards the Local Development of Multicultural Co-living" was submitted to the government. However, the multicultural co-living initiative still lacks substantial policies for immigration, social integration, and multiculturalism. A primary problem is that the government delegates actual support for and handling of foreign nationals living in Japan to local governments and nongovernmental and nonprofit organizations (Iwabuchi 2010). Hence, the multicultural co-living discussion is not concerned with the issues that need to be handled by national policy such as fair recognition of cultural differences and the development of related educational curriculums, antiracism campaigns, and media services that provide more spaces for diverse concerns and voices.

In relation to this, the discussion of multicultural co-living has a fundamental drawback in its bipolarized conception of "Japanese" and "foreigner," which defines "Japanese" in an exclusive and homogenizing manner and sidelines the appreciation of existing cultural diversity within Japan. The target group of multicultural co-living is identified as "foreigners as local residents." This conception neither properly recognizes the growing multicultural situation as a national matter nor attests to the inclusion of those with cultural differences as members of the national society. Also overlooked by the conception are cultural differences of long-standing ethno-racially marginalized people, including those who have Japanese nationalities by birth or by naturalization, as the notion of the "foreigner" in the multicultural co-living policy discussion tends to focus on recent migrants of non-Japanese nationality. The multicultural co-living policy discussion thus evades the vital question of who are Japanese citizens, proper members of society, and reinforces the rigid boundary between "Japanese" and "foreigners," whereby the engagement with cultural diversity within Japan is superseded by the advancement of international cultural exchange between "Japanese" and "foreigners."[11] In this point, multicultural co-living co-opts with the Cool Japan aspiration. The dissemination of attractive Japanese cultures is, as seen in the above statement, supposed to promote international cultural exchange, but in reality it aims to encourage foreigners to deepen their appreciation of Japanese culture. This kind of international exchange is further expected to incite foreigners' interest in visiting, traveling, and staying in Japan. And this is occasionally regarded as a type of international cultural exchange to be facilitated by a multicultural co-living program that local governments and universities promote.[12] Policy concerns of multicultural co-living and cool Japan conjointly advance an international cultural exchange based on the bipolarized notion of the Japanese and the foreigner and interact to overshadow attention to existing cultural diversity within Japan.

The policy discussion of creative industries has pointed out the significance of fostering cultural diversity for their developments (e.g., Florida 2002). In Japan, this issue is approached in terms of accepting foreign talents from overseas. In 2014, the Japanese government and METI started seriously discussing easing the granting of a long-stay visa to talented creators as part of the Cool Japan project. This is in line with the global tendency of eagerly accepting talented and creative workers useful to the national economy while strictly regulating the intake of other kinds of migrants. Such a selective policy will engender a new social and cultural hierarchy based on usefulness for the national economy. This is shown by the simultaneously ongoing discussion of the acceptance of foreign temporary labor from Asian regions for construction work for the Tokyo 2020 Olympics, the event that very much will be overlapping the Cool Japan projects. How the policy discussion of accepting "beneficial" foreigners for the Cool Japan project will be implemented and how many people will actually enter Japan through this scheme remains to be seen. In any case, a watchful eye needs to be kept on what sort of cultural diversity is encouraged and tolerated with a stress on talent and excellence that meets the demand of creative industries and whether and how it has an impact on the recognition and inclusion of marginalized diversity in Japan.[13]

ENGAGING WITH "CULTURE" FOR THE PUBLIC INTEREST

Raymond Williams (1984, 3–5) draws a distinction between cultural policies proper and cultural policies as display, as Jim McGuigan (2004) reminds us. Cultural policy proper is concerned with social democratization in terms of support for art and media regulation designed to counter the kind of penetrating market forces that tend to marginalize unprofitable cultural forms and the expressions of minority groups. Additionally, social democratization encompasses efforts aimed at the construction of open and dialogic cultural identities that go well beyond the constraints of the national imaginary. Cultural policy as display is "the public pomp of a particular social order" (Williams 1984, 3). This form of cultural policy is typically put on display by a given national event and ceremony in order to achieve "national aggrandizement."

Cultural policy as display also takes the form of an "economic reductionism of culture" that aims to promote domestic business opportunities and economic growth. While cultural policy can no longer effectively be developed without considering the role played by commercialized cultures in the public sphere, the two forms of cultural policy as display have been well integrated inasmuch as the state is trying to claim its regulating power by collaborating with private corporations.

A growing interest in national branding in Japan's Cool Japan policy shows how the two forms of cultural policy as display have been expediently integrated for the sake of the national interests, which does not correspond to or even suppresses crucial questions of who is the actual beneficiary and what is the democratizing potential of the promotion of media culture. The discursive formation focusing on the use of culture to enhance national interests conceals rather than reveals more imperative issues to be tackled within the era of globalization. There is no sign that the promotion of a nation branding policy accompanies engagement with the promotion of cross-border dialogue over transnationally shared issues as well as the democratizing possibility in terms of the recognition and treatment of ethno-racial differences. We need to put in the foreground the fundamental question about "the public good—this, understood as distinct from the political objectives of governments or the commercial objectives of the cultural industries" (Turner 2011, 696), in the discussion of cultural policy in Japan.

One crucial issue that the Japanese case highlights is the necessity of taking seriously the *domestic* implications of public/cultural diplomacy in order to promote cultural exchange and cross-border dialogue beyond the reinforcement of a homogenized and exclusive understanding of national culture. Recent discussion of public/cultural diplomacy underscores the significance of encouraging domestic publics to learn about and listen to others rather than merely project an image of itself (Holden 2013, 11). Learning about others, however, requires people to unlearn a predefined framework of knowing about "us" and "them" and rethink why and how "us" has been perceived in a way so as not to embrace "them" as being with and part of "us." Hence the domestic exercise of cultural/public diplomacy should elucidate what is yet unknown about "us," about "them," and about the relationship between "us" and "them" in terms of transnationally shared problems, historical narratives, and culturally diverse compositions of a nation. It does not negate the objective of cultural policy to promote national interests but expands the scope of national interests in a more open, dialogic, and inclusive way beyond the pursuit of narrowly focused economic and political objectives. Such is a cultural policy that engages with the public interest.

NOTES

1. See www.bunka.go.jp/1kokusai/kokusaikondankaihoukoku.html.

2. See MOFA's official web page: www.mofa.go.jp/policy/culture/exchange/pop/.

3. A TV program titled *Cool Japan* (NHK BS2) also started in 2006.

4. For example, see www.meti.go.jp/policy/mono_info_service/mono/creative/fy23_creative_report_r.pdf and www.bunka.go.jp/bunkashingikai/seisaku/10_06/pdf/shiryo_2.pdf.

5. This is also related to the fact that Japanese media and cultural industries have developed due to the great efforts made by media creators and corporations without the help of the state's promotion policy in the postwar era. For example, there has been no quota policy of regulating the import of foreign TV programs (as is also the case with Hong Kong), but the Japanese domestic TV market became nearly self-sufficient in the early 1970s. Media and cultural industries in Japan have a sense of pride that they have developed creative-production capacity by themselves and thus are cynical of the state's capacity to understand the process of media culture production, even holding a sense of antipathy toward the incorporation of media culture into the national strategy of Cool Japan. The state's involvement itself is considered "uncool."

6. It is against this background that many younger creators became furious with the comment made by Akimoto Yasushi in 2013. Akimoto is a prominent producer of media cultures such as TV programs and idols, including AKB48. In 2013, he was appointed as a member of the Council for the Promotion of Cool Japan. His willingness to participate in the national project of Cool Japan itself surprised many (as it is considered uncool), but his comment at the meeting was even more surprising and disappointed many creators. Akimoto made a comment that if there is not much of a budget for the promotion of Cool Japan, a team of first-class creators should be formed who would be happy to work for the Cool Japan project without any payment. He stated that everyone should be willing to work for the national strategy to rescue Japan in the age of the global competition of selling national culture. While his call for free labor was not made to all creators but to creators on the top, it immediately received much criticism and stirred up a sense of distrust against the eminent creators involved in cultural policy discussion on the Internet, especially among younger creators. And it is also guessed that Akimoto's seemingly passionate devotion to the national strategy of promoting Cool Japan likely masks the profits that he will make in the long run.

7. For the critique of creative industries in general, see Miller (2004).

8. When McDonald's ran its Kitty dolls campaign in 2000, it was reported that children from rural parts of China worked at the factory in Shenzen for fifteen hours a day and for the extremely low wage of twenty-one yen per hour (Takahashi 2001).

9. See www.kokusai-senryaku.ynu.ac.jp/sympo/pdf/20130125/09_saiki.pdf.

10. See www.e-stat.go.jp/SG1/estat/List.do?lid=000001118467.

11. This point is closely related to the fact that multicultural co-living has been developed as an extension of the "local internationalization" policy in the 1990s, through which the national government aimed to support local governments in accommodating the increasing number of foreigners staying and living in their constituency with a stated aim of smoothing international cultural exchange within Japan (see Iwabuchi 2010).

12. For example, see the Kanazawa municipal government's project of revitalization of the city: www4.city.kanazawa.lg.jp/11001/shiminkikou/shiminnkikou9/bosyuu.html. As for a university curriculum: info.bgu.ac.jp/faculty/foreign/english-education/.

13. See Hesmondhalgh (2013, 174–76) for a critique of an optimistic discussion that creative industries are not supposed to discriminate against people and should include more socioculturally marginalized people than other sectors.

Chapter Three

Lost in Trans-Nation

Post-Orientalism and the Actually Existing Multicultural Reality

The ascent of Japanese and other East Asian media culture is one conspicuous facet of media globalization that we have witnessed in the last two decades. While this testifies to the substantial advancement of production capacity of those countries, the global circulation of these media cultures has been facilitated by the mounting transnational alliance of media culture industries with the United States as the pivotal center. Hollywood's distribution networks are, for example, indispensable to make the Pokémon animation series and films (distributed by Warner Bros.) and the anime films of Hayao Miyazaki (distributed by Disney) a global culture. Moreover, the Pokémon anime series and movies that audiences around the world enjoy have been "Americanized," a process that involves removing some of their "Japaneseness" to make them more acceptable to global audiences from the perspective of American producers (see Allison 2006; Tobin 2004).

In turn, Hollywood has also been accommodating itself with the rise of Asian media culture production and lucrative markets so as to make its products more internationally oriented. Hollywood has been actively incorporating the strength of East Asian media culture production through the employment of directors and actors such as John Woo, Ang Lee, Jackie Chan, Zhang Ziyi, and Lee Byung-hun, and the remaking of Japanese, South Korean, and Hong Kong films such as *The Grudge*, *Shall We Dance*, *Infernal Affairs*, and *My Sassy Girl*. Hollywood also actively (co)produces and distributes Asia-related films such as *Hero*, *Crouching Tiger, Hidden Dragon*, *Kung Fu Hustle*, *The Last Samurai*, and *Memoirs of a Geisha*. In addition,

Hollywood studios are now actively producing "Asian" media cultures by setting up local branches in prosperous Asian cities.

It could be argued that Hollywood's embracing of Asia shows lingering uneven power relations between the United States and Asia, since "Asian" contents need to be modified to the taste and style of Hollywood, for which Western markets are still the most significant, even though its target audiences are becoming more global than before. However, the power relations in the global cultural economy have become more entangled than a Manichean picture of America-Asia. We should not dismiss the transformation of "America" either, in which "Asia" has come to occupy a significant part and Asian players are actively and cooperatively exploiting the opportunity to reach global markets. In this context, the rise of Asian media cultures neither fundamentally challenges the global cultural power configuration nor is simply subjugated by it.

A more complicated issue is that Hollywood's turn to Asia and the rise of Asia does not end the representation of Orientalist stereotypical images of Asian cultures and societies. The award-winning film *Lost in Translation* (*LIT* hereafter) is a case in point. The film attracted acclaim as well as criticism. While many praised the film's representation of modern people's sense of loss, critics differed over the film's representation of Tokyo, the city that constitutes a main character in the film. Some negative criticism centers on the film's effortless uses of Tokyo and of wider Japan to dramatize the sense of disorientation experienced by two privileged Americans. Highlighted here is the issue of whether and how the Western Orientalist gaze is still constitutive of the modish urban imaginary of Tokyo. This is certainly an intriguing question, but we need to have a wider scope of investigation to come to grips with it. This chapter will discuss how the urban imaginary of Tokyo that *LIT* represents as well as critical responses to it overtly and covertly show—and suppress—some of the emerging issues that Tokyo and Japan face in the era of globalization. The main question is how *LIT* and the responses to it in Japan illuminate issues such as the loss of idiosyncrasy of non-Western modernity that Japan has long enjoyed, post-(self-)Orientalist cultural othering, the transnational alliance of media and cultural industries, and global cultural economy of branding the nation through media culture, at the expense of the issue of the intensification of migration and multicultural situations in the urban space of Japan. I will suggest that, although the two main characters are lost in translation in the Tokyo setting, both *LIT* and Japanese responses to the film are, in different manners, lost in an ostensible shift in the geocultural configuration in a globalized world and that, more crucially, both are likewise lost in the actuality of Tokyo—and, indeed, Japan—and its populace, which is being radically transformed by intensifying transnational flows of people, capital, and media imagery.

POST-ORIENTALISM?

LIT has been acclaimed as a subtle narrative of modern lonesomeness and disorientation, empathetically and comically depicting two Americans—Bob, a middle-aged movie star, and Charlotte, a newly married Yale graduate—who share a time of bewilderment in a hypermodern foreign city, Tokyo. Being jetlagged and situated in a strange culture, they find their existential disorientation intensified and gradually fall for each other in a transient intimate relationship. Weary of being confused by unworkable cultural translation, Bob is stuck in a highly modern luxurious hotel that features seemingly familiar yet actually weird settings, such as a New York–style bar and an indoor pool. Together with Charlotte, he exits the hotel and starts adventuring in night spots in Tokyo's entertainment district. They finally find the determination to enter into a new stage of life. This emotional development is symbolized by the contrast between the opening scene and the closing scene, both of which depict the movie star getting into a taxi. The film opens with Bob's arrival in Shinjuku and his immediate bewilderment at a glittering, neon-lit street in the dark night. In the film's closing scenes, which take place as the daytime sky clears, he departs for the airport after uttering some perhaps heartwarming words into Charlotte's ear—words that bring tears to her eyes.

The director of the film, Sofia Coppola, who had experienced life in Tokyo, tries to make the best of its urban appeal and its bizarreness to enhance the sense of disorientation experienced by modern Americans who are lost in cultural translation. In terms of American imaginaries, this film's representation of urban life differs from, say, the corresponding representations in *Bladerunner* or in other science-fiction films that treat Tokyo-like cities as chaotic, futuristic megametropolises and that do so in a postmodern, techno-Orientalist manner (see Yoshimoto 1989; Morley and Robins 1995). *LIT*'s Tokyo is relatively mundane, flat, and hip. Coppola has repeatedly stated in various media interviews that she lived, worked, and played around in Tokyo and that she very much loves the city. She has stated, also, that she wanted to show Tokyo as she likes it. Apart from some scenes of Kyoto and of Buddhist temples in Tokyo, the urban scenes represented in the film are mostly evocative of major amusement districts such as Shinjuku and Shibuya: glittering neon lights, five-star hotels, hotel bars, subway, comic books, game centers, pachinko parlors, karaoke, strip bars, *shabu-shabu* (thin slices of beef parboiled in hot soup) and sushi restaurants, swimming pools, gyms, hospitals, election campaigns, and TV variety shows. The film represents these sites as components of modern urban life but stresses an inexplicable difference between Japanese urban life and American urban life. Bob describes Tokyo to his wife on the phone by noting, "It's very different." And Coppola herself stated, "I really want to do a movie here someday. I just loved the way visually it looks and the mood. I've never been in another place where I really felt like it's another planet" (Allen 2003). The film is "a valentine to Tokyo," she admitted—a valentine that expresses not Coppola's celebration of Tokyo as an ideal global city but her fascination with Tokyo's hypermodern bizarreness in the eyes of Americans.

In this respect, the film has attracted favorable responses as well as severe criticism. Some reviewers have approved of Coppola's Tokyo because, as they argue, the film depicts ordinary urban scenes in neither an idealized nor a degrading manner. Other reviewers have voiced their dislike of Coppola's Tokyo because, from their perspective, it is culturally insensitive and even racist toward people in Tokyo and, by extension, toward people in Japan.[1] Actually, most negative criticism that reviewers leveled against the film hinged less on the sites that Coppola chose to represent than on the classical Western Orientalism that she used to represent not only these sites but the people and the culture of Japan as well. By comically portraying the two Americans' encounters with a sensationally weird culture, people, and mode of urbanity in order to amplify the former's sense of loss and anguish, director Sofia Coppola has simplistically exploited Tokyo in a manner that haughtily mocks the people and the culture of Japan. Bob's linguistically and culturally incomprehensible encounters with Japanese people such as advertising companies' employees, the companies' clients, a TV comedian, and a prostitute are played for laughs. These representations can be read as testimony to the arrogance of Americans who make no effort to understand the language, culture, and people of Japan.

A well-known nonfiction writer, Sawaki Kotaro (2004), wrote that the film superficially depicts Japanese as completely stupid but that, on a more substantive level, the director unintentionally reveals the stupidity of Americans insofar as they do not even try to understand different languages and cultures. Considering this criticism in relation to the ethnocentrism characteristic of the United States in its war in Iraq, Sawaki concludes that Americans seem to think that if they do not understand others, the others must be to blame. Sawaki's criticism is well taken. Indeed, Coppola appears to be attracted to Japan's weird cultural dislocation of the West in the East and the traditional in the modern—as in a familiar Orientalist narrative. More important is Coppola's apparent lack of interest in depicting the possibility of, and indeed any attempt of, cross-cultural understanding or dialogue between Americans and Japanese. The film offers audiences no English translation of some key Japanese dialogue that highlights the cultural incomprehension. This untranslated dialogue effectively shows the real difficulty of interpersonal communication in an unknown language by urging English-language viewers to experience the sense of being lost in cultural miscommunication. However, what does concerns Coppola is not the engagement with the difficulty of cultural-linguistic translation but the comical representation of complete unintelligibility that Bob experiences in his encounter with Japanese people who look cheerfully and/or ceremoniously thoughtless. Bob is totally indifferent to the people, language, and culture of Japan, and without making any effort to understand them, he soon becomes so frustrated with the subsequent cultural unintelligibility that he tries to leave Japan and return home as soon as possible. There is certainly no attempt made to look at intercultural encounter from the other side, as Japanese people are just props to enhance Bob's sense of being lost in translation.

TRANSNATIONAL INDIFFERENCE IN A GLOBALIZED WORLD

Nevertheless, the criticism that these representations are ethnocentric and Orientalist somewhat misses the point. This criticism is based on the assumption that the film should deal with international or intercultural encounters between Japan and the United States and that, therefore, Americans must strive to understand cultural difference and look at themselves self-reflexively. Sawaki is well known for his travelogue about backpacking from Hong Kong to Turkey, and he tries to find in Coppola's film the moment of self-reflexive intercultural encounter that he experienced as an Asian backpacker. However, it is precisely this beside-the-mark expectation that actually disturbs him and evokes a strong sense of rejection within him. What Sawaki fails to grasp is that the film is not about a homesick type of desolation caused by a "the West meets the Rest" intercultural encounter but about a transnational dislocation involving accidental tourists whose sense of loss occurs in a crucial stage of life and is exacerbated by the perceived strangeness of their surroundings. Coppola's fascination with Tokyo diverges from intercultural Orientalism in this regard. One does not attempt to understand or evaluate cultural difference from one's own cultural standard; rather, one just stands in open-mouthed amazement at the encounter with other cultures. In *LIT*, Bob is too mentally distressed to appreciate cultural difference or pursue cultural dialogue. Being located in a foreign megacity is mental torture because its highly consumerist gaudiness and its ceaseless bustle further his sense of emptiness. Yet, the city is also a rite of passage to be overcome, as the last scene implies. While being indifferent to this other culture called "Japan," Bob cannot help but be more self-reflexive in his transient transnational dislocation.

For this cinematic imaginary, a strange place needs to be not premodern but highly modern yet highly different, highly affluent yet highly empty, highly global yet highly particularistic. In this way, Tokyo urbanity is appreciated precisely as a kind of globality—as possessing characteristics in common with those of major American cities—and this appreciation of commonality is fundamentally different from an Orientalist gaze on Tokyo or Japan. This imaginary does not devalue the other culture as "inferior" or "less developed" within an uneven bilateral relationship; rather, a spatial difference is explicated by situating two cultures on the same temporal level in the late modern capitalist world. In this sense, although the film's urban location for Coppola had to be Tokyo, it could actually be anywhere. This ambivalent specificity of Tokyo urbanity might also be a source of irritation for Japanese viewers. As the film makes no attempt either to understand Japan's cultural difference or to depict any Japanese subjectivity, it leaves a crucial question in some viewers' minds: why Tokyo? Even if an elegant hotel bar, the New York Bar, club culture, karaoke, and eccentric media entertainment impress the director as constitutive of Japanese cultural modernity's bizarreness, it is widely recognized now that these characteristics are no longer unique to Tokyo. This acclaimed Hollywood film's representations of Tokyo offend—rather than please—some people in Japan because Coppola's filmed fascination with Tokyo, by not addressing the protagonists' (mis)understanding of either Tokyo culture or Tokyo people, illuminates the fact that Tokyo no longer enjoys its once spectacular position as an exemplary non-Western icon in the Western imagination.[2]

The protagonists' lack of interest in bridging the cultural gap, I suggest, corresponds to the wider shift from the international economy of ethnocentric Orientalism to the transnational economy of self-absorbed indifference in a globalized world; in other words, the film addresses the issue of local specificity not so much in terms of the relationship between national uniqueness and Western cultural hegemony as of bizarre resemblance in a globalized world, which has been generated by transnational flows of capital, commodified culture, and imagery. Many places around the world can express this consumerist version of local specificity because so many places around the world share the modes of urban culture and are thus substitutable for one another. While intercultural Orientalism undermines the claim that Westerners misunderstand the Japanese and that distorted images of Japan prevail in the West, *LIT*'s transnational indifference suggests that "they" do not even try to understand "us." To depict a scenario in which Americans cast a gaze of indifference upon Tokyo is to suggest, as I have mentioned, that any non-Western megacity can replace not only Tokyo but Japan as well. Indeed, some Japanese moviegoers might feel profound frustration when a Western film about Japanese culture expresses neither the West's respect for nor the West's surprise at—nor even the West's antagonism toward—Japan. A comparison of *LIT* with the 1991 Hollywood film *Black Rain* clarifies the point. *Black Rain* represents both the vulgarity of the Osaka area and American antagonistic views of Japan. The film's main theme concerns a clash that pits Japanese and Americans against each other and stems from the rise of Japanese economic power at that time. In this regard, the textuality of *LIT* merits examination in light of Japan's changing global position over the last decade or so—change that is marked by Japan's long-lasting socioeconomic decline and loss of self-confidence.

THE DECADES OF LOSS: FROM "INTERNATIONALIZATION" TO "GLOBALIZATION"

What has become apparent in the last two decades since early 1990s, which is often called "the two decades of loss" (*ushinawareta nijûnen*), is that Japan is no longer a spectacular, uniquely unique non-Western modern nation but has become quite an ordinary one; ordinary in the sense that it follows a path similar to Euro-American developed nations toward facing the limits of economic progress with various kinds of socioeconomic anxiety, contradiction, and disintegration—such as a widening gap between the haves and the have-nots, and the increasing sense of insecurity caused by unemployment and the diminution of the social welfare system—defying resolution amid a process of gradual decline.

It is perhaps not incidental at all that the end of the Cold War coincided with the end of Japan's postwar rise insofar as Japan was perhaps the greatest beneficiary of American Cold War policy. While the post–Cold War era has witnessed many expressions of hitherto suppressed "memory wars" (Huyssen 2003), the memory of the Cold War in Japan is associated exclusively with economic miracle and consumer enjoyment. In the era of neoliberal globalization, Japan has to renew its path for the future. Yet transnational capital does not easily allow Japan to take control of its own path, especially when Japan's bubble economy has collapsed and when other Asian countries have significantly developed their economic powers.

Japan's loss of confidence has accompanied a change in the discourse of Japan's national identity. Japan is infamous for being excessively preoccupied with its own cultural uniqueness. *Nihonjinron* literature explains Japanese people and culture in essentialist terms, and its popularity is indicative of the strong interest within Japan to identify and to explain Japanese uniqueness. Studies show how Japanese national-cultural identity has been constructed through a conscious self-Orientalizing discourse, a narrative that, at once, testifies to subtle exploitation of and deep complicity with Western Orientalist discourses (Iwabuchi 1994). Japan is represented and represents itself as culturally and racially homogeneous and uniquely particularistic by way of a strategic binary opposition between two imaginary cultural entities, "Japan" and "the West."[3] In the decade after Japan became an economic superpower (a period when the nationalist slogan of *kokusaika*, "internationalization," became prevalent in Japan), the Japanese government and Japanese companies devoted themselves to furthering Japan's national interests through competition in the international arena. This process coincided with a dramatic increase in opportunities for Japanese to establish contact with foreign—predominantly Western—people and cultures both inside Japan and abroad. Backed by the strong Japanese economy and the relative decline of American power, the self-Orientalizing *nihonjinron* literature became a popular commodity, one through which the Japanese populace could confidently explain the distinctive characteristics of Japanese culture and society without undermining the demarcation between "us" and "them" (Iwabuchi 1994). This trend culminated, in the 1980s, with Japan's accession to the position of an economically powerful nation-state (Kondo 1997, 84), shortly before the aforementioned film *Black Rain* was produced.

The internationalist *nihonjinron* discourse has dropped away since the collapse of Japan's bubble economy in the early 1990s and the subsequent entrenchment of social malaise. Since then Japan has witnessed an apparently decisive structural breakdown that corresponded to changes in such Japanese institutions as the state bureaucracy, corporate organization, the education system, and family relationships. A prolonged economic recession and incidents such as the Kobe earthquake, an increasing number of brutal crimes committed by teenagers, and the Aum Shinrikyô nerve-gas attacks in the Tokyo subway system further deepened the sense of crisis and pessimism. These changes were accompanied by the rapid development of globalization, in which transborder flows and connections among capital, people, and media accelerated at an unprecedented scale and speed. In this context, the keyword in the discussion of Japan's place in the world shifted from "international" to "global."[4] As the then popular term *global standard* exemplifies, Japanese discourses on globalization have most notably revolved around the necessity for Japan to readjust itself to the new U.S.-led global economic order. The usage of *global* and *globalization* in Japan thus implies a more passive and less confident condition than the older term did, signifying that Japan is in a crisis of decay. Saskia Sassen might still call Tokyo a global city, as she does in her 1996 book, but people's perceptions are far more negative within Japan itself. A useful source of understanding in this regard is a comparative survey that the research institute of Japan's biggest advertising company, Dentsu, conducted between October and November 2001. Focusing on perceptions of globalization in Japan, the United States, the United Kingdom, France, and Germany, the survey found that people in other countries tended to have rather optimistic views on globalization. However, nearly 60 percent of Japanese people tended to stress globalization's negative effects such as widening economic gap and employment insecurity and express personal anxiety about these effects (Takahashi 2003).

In this context, we have observed the explosion of nationalistic discourses in various forms, though Japan no longer claims cultural distinctiveness and superiority founded on economic power since the mid-1990s. Many attempts have been made to (re)discover the merit and virtue of Japan: nostalgia for past glory, reactive discourses that aim to revise history textbooks to counter the "self-tormenting" view of Japan's modern history of imperialism and colonialism in Asia, and the state's emphasis on teaching Japanese children more about their traditions and instilling patriotic sentiments. Indeed, the 1990s has been marked as the decade of the upsurge of neonationalism (see Abe 2001; Yoda 2000). However, this is a clear testimony that the socioeconomic and geopolitical changes have deprived *nihonjinron* discourse of its explanatory power—a power that is based on an internationalist binary between Japan and the West. This loss of explanatory power characterizes not just discourse in Japan but also discourse in the West, as the two are in a complicit relationship with each other. *LIT* testifies to the end of that complicity, showing a shift toward transnational indifference. It is no longer possible for an essentialist discourse on Japanese national identity to effectively use the power of the Western Orientalist gaze for the affirmation of Japan's high, and unique, international standing.

EMBRACING COOL JAPAN

This does not mean, however, that Tokyo and Japan are entirely losing international drawing power. As discussed earlier, *LIT*'s and Coppola's transnational indifference is accompanied by the fascination with the urban cultural scene of Tokyo. This is, it can be argued, something indicative of the recent praise of Japan's "cool culture" and encourages us to look at the wider context in which *LIT* was produced and decoded. While Hollywood's active embracing of "East Asia," hence "Japan," in its production and marketing process has been engendered by the boosting of the transnational collaboration among media and cultural industries, co-occurring with it is, as discussed in the previous two chapters, the highlighting of the renewed significance of the nation and its culture in the inter-national arena. Especially relevant here is the increasing interest in branding the nation through media and consumer cultures in a metropolis, which has been promoted by (transnational) media and cultural industries, as well as by the states. Against this background, *LIT* has acquired extra positive meanings and interpretations in Japan.

The recent spike in Hollywood films representing and involving Japan needs to be considered in light of the above-mentioned structural transformation, but such a complication does not actually matter much in the emerging discourse of branding the nation as it predominantly construes the phenomenon in a way to confirm the rise of "Cool Japan." For example, the director of the Japan Information Center of the Consulate General of Japan stated in New York in 2003 that "many popular Japanese or Japan-inspired movies—

such as *The Ring, Kill Bill, Lost in Translation, The Last Samurai*, and *The Matrix*—are directly influenced by samurai, karaoke, anime and manga" and that "Japan's increasing cultural influence shows the growth of Japan's soft power" (Consulate-General of Japan in New York 2004). Likewise, *Newsweek Japan* (March 3, 2004) carried a feature story titled "Hollywood Loves Japan," placing a scene from *LIT* on the issue's cover. It discussed Japan's increasing cultural power by referring to *The Last Samurai, Kill Bill*, the remake of *The Ring*, and *LIT*, but without seriously considering the transmuting configuration of Hollywood's "fascination with Japan." It seems that the fact of Hollywood films' embracing Japanese themes is only important in playing to national vanity.

Tourism is one of the strategically significant industries for nation branding. Both the Japanese government and the Tokyo metropolitan government are trying to attract more foreign tourists to Japan and, in particular, to Tokyo. While Tokyo cannot compete with Kyoto's traditional attractions and heritage industry, Tokyo's appeal is to be found in a subtle combination of the traditional and the (super)modern within a highly consumerist urban setting. For example, Tokyo attracts no small number of tourists from East Asia who like to experience Tokyo as depicted in popular TV drama series (Lee 2004). The newly developed bay area Odaiba is a popular destination that hosts a particularly popular TV station (Fuji TV) and a famous Ferris wheel. Another attraction is made up of the traditional shopping, entertainment, and residential districts of Tokyo. Also attractive to visitors' eyes is karaoke, game centers, and dance clubs, all of which are subtly depicted in *LIT*. In effect, the film has indirectly encouraged Japanese organizations to enhance their own agenda for attracting international tourism. The Japanese National Tourist Organization treated the film's popularity as an opportunity to promote tourism across Japan as well as in Tokyo. The organization made a campaign of "Yokoso Japan: *Lost in Translation* Packages," through which visitors could enjoy the sites that appeared in the film: "Japan welcomes tourists enchanted by the acclaimed film *Lost in Translation.*"

Interestingly, Sawaki's (2004) anger against *LIT* was also tempered by learning that the luxurious hotel in Shinjuku that had served as the film's main shooting location was now a popular destination for American celebrities. "Surely the hotel, and its bar in particular, is depicted quite attractively. If we regard the film as a promotional film of this hotel, perhaps we should not get so angry with its representation," Sawaki declared. The usefulness for nation branding perceived as such apparently relieves the national uneasiness that arises in the era of transnational indifference.

INTO THE CITY: UNREPRESENTED ACTUALITY
OF MULTICULTURAL POLITICS

National thinking persists in the era of globalization. This persistence helps explain the confusion in the film reviews of *LIT* between the representation of an urban space, Tokyo, and the representation of the national imaginary, Japan. This is again clearly the case with Sawaki's commentary, in which he exclusively calls into question the film's representation of Japan and the Japanese rather than the film's representation of Tokyo. This confusion is not just an issue of overgeneralization but also one of the imaginative confinement of "methodological nationalism" that presupposes "the self-evidence of a world ordered into nation-states" (Wimmer and Schiller 2002, 325), without which mutual cultural othering would be unworkable.

It can be argued that, in response to the relentless recurrence of the national, we should pay more attention to urban space to make sense of what is happening in the world today. The city and urban spaces can be considered sites of "actually existing" cultural multiplicity and negotiation that cannot easily be grasped by a container model of the nation, and we might better be able to foster alternative social imaginations by closely examining urban dynamics in all their complexity. While the arbitrariness of the nation is now well acknowledged, it tends to be understood mostly in terms of a necessary fiction of community, "as a community of fate, to be sustained in its essential unity through the course of historical time" (Robins 2000, 487). To grasp the actuality of society, we need to "extend our cultural and political concerns from the national question to the urban question":

> If the nation is fundamentally about belonging to an abstract community . . .
> then the urban arena is about immersion in a world of multiplicity, and impli-
> cates us in the dimension of embodied cultural experience. . . . The nation, we
> may say, is a space of identification and identity, whilst the city is an experien-
> tial and existential space. (Robins 2000, 489)

It is imperative that we grasp this point so as to fruitfully engage with the issues of "disordering transformations," such as issues of migration, transnationalization, and multiculturalism, because "they cannot be made sense of within the national mentality" (Robins 2000, 486). Likewise, Ien Ang distinguishes urban citizenship—"politics of presence" that "centers around the everyday pragmatic and affective dimensions of 'rights to the city'"—from national citizenship—"politics of representation" that is "generally defined in terms of a formal demarcation of national belonging (such as the possession of a passport and the ability to vote)" (Ang 2006, 33):

> While concepts of national citizenship are delimited in absolutist terms of
> inclusion and exclusion, urban citizenship encompasses the process of living

with difference, rather than its negation, handling actual heterogeneity rather
than imposing imaginary homogeneity or commonality. (39)

Politics of presence highlights how citizenship is actually practiced and
negotiated in the urban space, which is beyond reach at the level of national
representation.

Neither film critics such as Sawaki nor filmmakers such as Coppola appreciate the urgency of turning to urban space. Indeed, alongside Coppola's
fascination with Tokyo is *LIT*'s pronounced lack of interest in the lives of
Tokyo's people. The film certainly depicts Tokyo rather than Japan, urban
space rather than national culture, but, as I mentioned earlier, the film fails to
examine the diverse human subjects and interactions embraced by Tokyo.
This fatal exclusion significantly limits Coppola's urban imaginary and both
lends itself to and colludes with film critics' comments about intercultural
Orientalism, which prioritizes national culture and, thereby, encourages people to disregard the dynamics of urban space.

One significant aspect of Tokyo that is missing in the film is Tokyo's
growing diversity, which reflects the increasing number of migrants there
and the subsequent furthering of multicultural situations there. Given its
relatively small number of foreign residents and its highly restrictive policy
toward migrants, we cannot reasonably regard Tokyo as a global city that is
comparable to New York, London, or Sydney. Yet Tokyo remains one of the
most multicultural and transnational urban spaces in Japan. As pointed out in
the previous chapter, since the late 1980s, the number of migrants to Japan
drastically increased, owing to the strength of both the yen and the overall
economy, and the number of foreign-national residents in Japan has been
steadily increasing even after the collapse of the so-called bubble economy in
the early 1990s. By region, the largest number of foreign nationals live in
Tokyo, and the city's international marriages account for more than 10 percent of all marriages in Tokyo. Undoubtedly then, people residing in Tokyo
have more opportunities than people elsewhere in Japan to encounter foreign
residents. This was evident in a survey that the government office conducted
in 2001, which asked respondents to identify how frequently they would
encounter "foreigners": only 11 percent of Tokyo respondents replied "hardly ever," whereas 40 percent of respondents nationally replied "hardly ever."
And 77 percent of Tokyo respondents felt that their everyday lives were
affected by the growing number of foreign residents, whereas 54 percent
nationally felt the same way.

Not unlike Kevin Robins's London, Tokyo is full of multicultural and
transnational practices that encourage us to develop urban imaginaries as
alternatives to national ones. Yet, as is the case with many other major cities,
urban space is not a migrant heaven. It is a space where migrants access
greater opportunities as well as confront strident racism, xenophobia, and

other forms of exclusionary violence. This violence is an important issue because one of the most dreadful society-wide trends in modern Japan is the suppression, if not the erasure, of multicultural engagement at the societal level. Critics have widely observed that a public concern with social inclusion has been overwhelmed by the politics of exclusion in many parts of the world since the late 1990s and, even more conspicuously, since the September 11 attacks. As Graeme Turner (2003) argues in the Australian context, the discussion of multicultural politics and the subversive potential evoked by the notion of hybridity have rapidly receded in the twenty-first century. What has become prevalent in mainstream discourse is a pronounced desire to expand security and surveillance practices. The enemy against which the state has to defend the nation is not just an "axis of evil" that terrorizes civilized nations but also migrants and asylum seekers who are "invading" a nation from the outside and cultural others who are jeopardizing the nation's social cohesion and safety from the inside. And the megacity is the most vulnerable to such attacks, it is often argued, because suspects can easily sneak into and hide in the urban space.

We need to remember that Tokyo then had a most notorious nationalist governor, Shintaro Ishihara, who was reelected with strong support in 2011 (and he quit the governorship and moved back to national politics in the election in late 2012). Tokyo's metropolitan government takes a firm attitude to instill—through official notice to all schools—a sense of patriotism at the site of education. The notice mandates that Tokyo's schoolchildren and teachers hoist the national flag and sing the national anthem while standing up at school ceremonies. Those teachers who do not stand up to sing the national anthem are severely penalized. Furthermore, the increasing number of foreign residents has intensified popular anxiety about social security and about the rise of criminal activities by foreigners, especially in Tokyo. The Japanese media have long tended to treat foreign residents as social problems or as threats to the Japanese community. This tendency became especially conspicuous in the late 1980s, when Japan experienced a dramatic increase in the number of temporary and permanent migrants from Asia. There was, at that time, some concern over how and, indeed, whether Japan could become a multiracial nation.[5] There was massive social discussion as to whether or not Japan should take in migrants, and the media covered the issues of migrants' poor working conditions in Japan, migrants' lives in Japan, and the racial discrimination that migrants faced in Japan. Many films addressed the issues of Asian migrants, of international marriages between Japanese and non-Japanese, of foreign students in Japan, and of Japan's reliance on foreigners as cheap labor. However, while the number of foreign-national residents has been steadily increasing, the Japanese media no longer pay much attention to the above issues in the new millennium, which have ceded place to issues concerning the threat of crime and of illegal migrants to society and community.

Migrants from China in particular have attracted significant public attention regarding the growth in crimes committed by foreign nationals. Racist comments made in 2000 by Tokyo governor Shintaro Ishihara exemplify such concerns. He attributed the rise of crime, in large part, to the rise of illegal Chinese migrants. The Japanese media repeatedly reported the increase in—and the viciousness of—crimes committed by foreigners, but the media, rather than carefully examine the accuracy of the statistics, uncritically accepted as truth the information that law enforcement disseminated (Morris-Suzuki 2003). In truth, the number of crimes that foreigners commit in Japan constitutes an insignificant proportion of the total number of crimes (Utsumi et al. 2001). But it is not unusual for people to believe what they want to believe, and the news media panders to this tendency. News reports regularly describe suspects as foreign or as being "of foreign appearance," even though there is no clear evidence to support these assertions, thereby reproducing and reinforcing the wider public's association of foreigners with crime and danger. The Japanese media's demonizing of foreigners effectively engenders Japan's widely felt sense of social distress. This distress not only centers on crime but also on unemployment, terrorism, the breakdown of the education system, and the drastic, looming decline in postretirement pensions. Given that people are not offered comprehensive analyses of these globally shared social issues, repeated news reports on foreigners' crimes make people apt to attribute the cause of anxiety to palpable villains that threaten "our" national communities and that should therefore be expelled from the nation. The practice of exclusion evokes a highly romanticized longing for a safe and caring community (Bauman 2001).

According to the above-mentioned comparative survey on globalization-related issues, people in Japan cited the increase of foreigners' criminal activities as the most worrisome effect of globalization. According to a survey by the government, the percentage of people who responded positively to the question of whether or not the human rights of foreign-national residents should be respected and protected decreased from 65.5 percent in 1997 to 54 percent in 2003 (*Asahi Shinbun*, April 13, 2003). In this same survey, 73 percent of Tokyo residents expressed concern with foreign labor issues, whereas nationally, only 49 percent expressed the same concern. These statistics reflect the Japanese people's growing anxiety over illegal labor: 60 percent of Tokyo residents worried about it and about associated crime, whereas nationally, 49 percent expressed the same worry. Apparently, actually existing multiculturalism is being lost not just in Coppola's transnational indifference but also in media-aggravated transnational anxiety.

BEYOND INTER-NATIONAL COMPLICITY

In the 1980s, Japanese researchers were vigorously studying Tokyo's city life. At that time, people around the world regarded Tokyo as the only non-Western global city of simulacra, boasting newly built postmodern buildings, highly consumerist entertainment districts, and amusement spaces, including Tokyo Disneyland (Wakabayashi 2005). Perceptions of Tokyo have changed since then, and *LIT*'s representation of Tokyo exemplifies the city's shift from a nowhere-but-Tokyo specificity to an anywhere-including-Tokyo generality. Tokyo might be losing some of its idiosyncrasies in the face of various kinds of intercity rivalry. Shanghai might have already become a much more stimulating place where privileged Americans can lose themselves in the spectacle of a West-East fusion. Seoul might become a center of digital media culture and signify a more stunning urban imaginary. At the same time, these losses make it no longer feasible to imagine Tokyo as the representative of a homogeneous nation that supports a Western imaginary of intercultural Orientalism.

Tokyo might still be lost in transnational flows and connections; already, Tokyo residents have registered a loss in their socioeconomic confidence, in the idiosyncrasy of Tokyo's non-Western modernity, and its imagined homogeneity. Yet, these very losses constitute a good opportunity for Tokyo to revive itself and to make its space more humane and inclusive. Sassen (2005, 89) argues that "large cities concentrate both the leading sectors of global capital and a growing share of disadvantaged population" and that, because of this concentration, "cities have become a strategic terrain for a whole series of conflicts and contradictions." Tokyo continues to be such a site, where multicultural co-living with marginalized and powerless people, whose full membership is not well recognized in the national framework, is mundanely practiced: "In so far as the sense of membership of these [various] communities is not subsumed under the national, it may well signal the possibility of a politics that, while transnational, is actually centered in concrete localities" (Sassen 2005, 92). As Mikio Wakabayashi (2005) points out, the post-1980s decline of Japan's urban studies on Tokyo has coincided with the upsurge of urban development in a self-contained theme-park-like style, which renders surrounding urban spaces into a "blank" by turning its back from the sociohistorical contexts and detaching itself from diverse people's everyday practices. Then it is to this kind of socially contextualized local politics that we need to turn our analytical and imaginative rigor in an attempt to comprehend the urban imaginary of Tokyo in its full sense.

Furthermore, Tokyo will remain a giant city that will accept more migrants for years to come. According to a UN Population Division report in 2000, Japan has to accept 610,000 migrants every year for another fifty years so as to maintain both the current labor force, which is aging, and the current level of economic activity. Japan, as one of the most aging populations in the world, also has to take in foreign laborers who will perform nursing duties specifically for elderly people. In addition, Tokyo will host the Olympic Games in 2020, and the acceptance of temporary labor from Asian regions is an imperative issue. These vast present and predicted changes serve as a reminder that, for people who are actually residing there, Tokyo cannot be the dizzying space devoid of local subjectivities that is represented in Coppola's cinematic imaginary. After all, it is precisely the impossibility of representing Tokyo in its actually existing multiplicity that both *LIT* and the various critical responses to the film reveal.

At the same time, we should not confine our critical interrogation of multicultural questions to the existing diversity in the urban space but engage with Orientalism's symbolic violence going beyond national borders. Film representations of *LIT* and the reaction against it in Japan testify to the lingering complicity between the Western representation of Japan and Japan's reaction/embracing of it. This time, we are urged to turn our attention more to what/who is not represented. A significant issue involved is the transnational complexity of (self-)Orientalism politics. It is often Asian Americans who clearly speak out in the forefront of contestations against the Hollywood representation of Japan. For them, the American representation of "them/there" has an even more direct impact on their sociocultural positioning within "us/here." As was also the case with other Japan-related films, such as *Rising Sun* or *Pearl Harbor*, that were criticized as racist, those most seriously offended by Hollywood's representation of cultural others are often people who, living within the United States, occupy its margins. This point suggests that the most strident objections to Orientalism tend to surface intrasocietally rather than inter-nationally. [6]

This is a good reminder that Orientalism should not be discussed in terms of uneven intercultural relations and encounters between discrete cultural entities should not be presumed as such. As Edward Said (1978) makes clear, it is through the discourse of Orientalism that such an imagining of culturally coherent entities and geography comes into being. And in many cases, as pointed out in chapter 1, when Western Orientalism discourses are countered by oriental Occidentalism or self-Orientalism, the two discourses are in collusion in terms of the mutual construction of culturally coherent entities. The hidden but most seriously injured of Orientalism is those who are minoritized in the imagined cultural entity. And this symbolic violence has become even more salient in the process of media and cultural globalization, which generates the inter-national administration of cultural diversity.

NOTES

1. See, for example, ABC dane.net, "Review of Lost in Translation," February 20, 2004, abcdane.net/archives/000877.html, and JTNews, reviews of *Lost in Translation*, www.jtnews.jp/cgi-bin/review.cgi?TITLE_NO=6374ABC, for various Japanese viewers' comments. For critical reviews, see, for example, Yoko Asahi, "'Lost in Translation' Insults Japanese," *Japan Today*, www.japantoday.com/e/, and Peter Brunette, "Sofia Coppola's Overly Subtle 'Lost in Translation,'" IndieWire, web.archive.org/web/20080313175023/http://www.indiewire.com/movies/movies_030917lost.html, which have critical responses from American viewers, including Asian/Japanese Americans.

2. These are in a sharp contrast to another American film, *Yakuza*, starring Robert Mitchum and Ken Takakura, which shows a great effort toward an intercultural understanding. Thanks to Peter Seelig for this suggestion.

3. This is not to say that "Asia" has no cultural significance in the construction of Japanese national identity. While Japan's construction of its national identity through the complicity between Western Orientalism and Japan's self-Orientalism is conspicuous, "Asia" has also overtly or covertly played a constitutive part. While "the West" played the role of the modern other to be emulated, "Asia" was cast as the image of Japan's past, a negative picture that tells of the extent to which Japan has been successfully modernized according to the Western standard.

4. According to *Asahi Shinbun*'s data base, the number of articles using the word *international* dropped from 1,104 in 1990 to 436 in 2002, while those using the word *global* rose from 42 to 510 in the same period.

5. For example, see "Nihon ga taminzoku kokka ni naru hi" [When Japan becomes a multiethnic nation], *Bessatsu Takarajima*, no. 106 (1990).

6. See Brunette, "Sofia Coppola's Overly Subtle 'Lost in Translation.'"

Chapter Four

Making It Multinational

Media Representation of Multicultural Japan

While cross-border flows and connections are increasingly becoming mundane, as discussed in chapter 1, there has been a market-driven propensity to make the banality of the nation more solid and deeply infiltrated into people's minds. A significant role in this development is the media spectacle of global events (especially sports) and inter-national gatherings of various kinds. The increasing prominence of an Olympiad framework of global cultural exchange has accompanied the entrenched permeation of an assumption that the world is the congregation of various nations, which urges people to display one's membership for participation in the global society. This chapter considers how this framework is applied to the representation of intensifying multicultural situations in Japan.

An apparent paradigm shift in the discourse on Japanese national identity from international(ization) to global(ization) has had a noticeable implication in the media representation of "foreigners" in Japan. On the one hand, as discussed in the previous chapter, the activation of people's border crossing has intensified anxiety about national communal security, and the mass media have tended to treat foreign residents as social problems and/or threats to the Japanese community. On the other hand, the Japanese media have also had an impetus to represent foreign residents as consumable signs through which the potentially threatening increase in the number of migrants and foreign nationals and their growing visibility in Japan can be translated into a controllable media spectacle. Through the examination of the representation of "ordinary foreigners" (*futsû no gaikokujin*) in a Japanese TV talk show, I will discuss how the pleasurable commodification of national belonging and cultural othering occurs, which contain the increasing presence and visibility of foreign-national residents in the mediated space. In this move, the borders between "us" and "them" are clearly redemarcated so as to subtly turn an intensifying multicultural situation into a multinational spectacle.

MEDIA REPRESENTATION OF FOREIGN-NATIONAL RESIDENTS IN THE AGE OF GLOBALIZATION

At least since the early 1960s, foreign-national people have appeared in the Japanese mass media as commentators and entertainers, but it was in the 1980s, the decade of "internationalization," that this tendency intensified and so-called *gaijin-tarento* (foreign celebrities) became media celebrities. They were mostly Caucasians from Western countries, predominantly the United States, and fluent in Japanese.[1] Their assigned task was, like the narrative in *nihonjinron*, to mark the uniqueness of Japan in entertaining ways. They were repeatedly asked to comment on Japanese culture or current affairs with a particular emphasis on the difference between Japan and the "Rest/West" (Hall 1992). *Gaijin-tarento*, on their side, subtly played their assigned role to satisfy the Japanese desire to be regarded as unique.

However, as *nihonjinron* discourses declined, the value of *gaijin-tarento* decreased. The increasing number of foreign nationals residing in Japan who, to an even more considerable degree, acquired Japanese cultural competence in terms of language skills and insights into Japanese culture and society also undermined the raison d'être of *gaijin-tarento*. The favored Japanese media commodity became the "ordinariness" of foreign residents. There emerged, for example, TV programs in which unknown foreigners contested with each other in singing Japanese songs that included *enka* (a ballady music of Japanese popular song full of melancholy) and those programs that described the everyday struggles of foreign brides in Japan. There was also a public TV commercial by the Japan Advertising Council in 2002 that featured an American woman who successfully worked as a landlady in Yamagata. In the ad, she stressed the traditional virtues of Japan, which many Japanese people seem to forget, with a statement that the Japanese are short of "Japan" (*Nipponjin niwa nihon ga tarinai*). These examples demonstrate that the *gaijin-tarento*'s role of highlighting Japan's distinctiveness had been replaced by the "ordinary" foreigner's gaze and body. Testifying to this development, there appeared a new type of TV talk show, *Kokoga hen dayo Nihonjin* (*KHN* hereafter), that featured the outspoken voices and opinions of foreign residents about Japan. As I discuss below, *KHN* displays an attempt to redefine "Japan" through the representation of Japan in/and the global society. What is crucial here is the fact that "ordinary foreigners" are required to be explicit about where they are from by showing their (non-Japanese) nationalities. A multinational spectacle is substituted for multicul-

tural politics whereby the issue of inclusion/exclusion in the Japanese imagined community is rendered irrelevant.

"ORDINARY FOREIGNERS" WANTED

After a few successful trials as a special program, *KHN* was broadcast as an
hour-long weekly program (at 10:00 p.m.) from October 1998 to March
2002. The program gained relatively high ratings in this time slot (around 15
percent on average). The show featured one hundred foreigners in a studio
audience who were willing to give their opinions on various topics. It usually
began with foreigners' statements expressing their sense of anger and frustration and the oddness they felt about Japanese sociocultural matters such as
racial discrimination, international marriage, school bullying, and animal
abuse. On the Japanese side, concerned persons and commentators (come-
dians, intellectuals, social critics, and so on) appeared in the studio and in
most cases agitated the discussion by refuting the foreigners' points in a
confrontational manner. As the producer stated, the target audience of this
program was those who did not have a critical awareness of the issues involved (*Asahi Shinbun*, May 22, 2001, evening ed.). The program did not
aim to offer rational, well-structured discussions but to provoke a quarrel
through an exaggerated and simplified comparison between "Japan and the
rest."[2]

The show apparently shares much with earlier media representations of
foreigners in terms of the attempt to discursively construct an exclusive
Japanese imagined community, but it also draws a clear line between them in
some respects. In an interview I conducted at TBS on January 19, 2001, the
producer told me that his idea for the show was originally inspired by *nihonjinron* literature, which he had enjoyed reading as a university student.[3] He
wanted to create a TV talk show that elucidated the distinctive traits of
Japanese society and culture by comparing them to those of other cultures
and nations. In implementing his idea, the producer stressed the significance
of featuring nameless foreigners. According to him, the newness of the program lay in the review of contemporary Japanese society through the opinions of foreigners who were living as ordinary residents in Japan. This was
necessitated by the steady increase in the number of foreign nationals residing there:

> I thought it was important to feature ordinary people from many parts of the
> world. There are now so many foreign nationals living in Japan. The situation
> is much different from before. I want to give them a space to express their
> views on issues about Japanese culture and society as well as the sense of
> frustration they feel while inhabiting Japan, which is something we should not
> easily dismiss.

Yet representing ordinary people's voices was apparently commercially significant in making the show appealing to Japanese audiences. It was assumed that since foreign discussants appearing on the show were "ordinary" people, their comments would be regarded as genuine, not deliberately exaggerated and contrived performances as was the case with *gaijin-tarento* (*Television*, February 26, 1999, 35–37). Moreover, convinced by the popularity of *nihonjinron*, the producer was quite sure that "Japanese people would like to listen to how foreigners perceive their society and culture" to confirm Japanese distinctiveness. The ordinariness of enraged foreigners was believed to ensure the authenticity of their voices, which in turn helped their utterances about Japan sound radical and fresh to viewers. The talk show format was seen as a strategically appropriate way to represent such voices and reconfirm the symbolic boundaries of "Japan" in a stimulating way. Ordinary foreign residents were regarded as an attractive commodity of alterity in a televised multicultural "safari park" where Japanese audiences could safely enjoy the spectacle of (sometimes scary) intercultural encounters through the screen.

The minimum requirement for foreign participants in *KHN* was that they possess oral language skills fluent enough to allow them to discuss various topics with their Japanese counterparts. In addition, the producer seemed to be uncomfortable with the fact that the foreign discussants often made other media appearances, taking advantage of their participation in the program. However, this should not be taken straightforwardly. What *ordinariness* meant to the producer was not at all self-evident. Whether or not the discussants were really nonprofessional, ordinary people did not seem to matter much to him; he was more concerned with making them look ordinary. Thus, the question to be investigated is how the program attempted to represent the ordinariness of foreign discussants to fit its commercial purpose.

While the talk show was expected to depict the spontaneous expressions of the discussants, the production side tightly controlled the content of *KHN*. The topics of each program were entirely decided by the production team, and discussants were asked to report their views and opinions in advance. Then the production side considered the desirable direction of the debate, who would make an interesting comment for the show, and what kinds of video images should be inserted in order to make the show most enjoyable. In the studio, the master of ceremonies, Kitano Takeshi, was informed in advance who would make the most stimulating comments on the topic and, therefore, who should be picked.

The lifeline of *KHN* was how to secure foreign-national residents who could make intriguing and stirring comments and compare Japan to their own countries. The program constantly inserted statements recruiting foreign discussants. According to the producer, some members of the foreign discussants were regularly switched out so the program would not fall into a rut.

Those whose presence and comments failed to enliven the discussion were apt to disappear from the program. Discussants who were able to make intriguing comments in the producer's favor continued to appear on the program, and some even became amateur media celebrities.

In relation to this, a talent agency, Inagawa Motoko Office (IMO), played a significant role in the recruitment and management of foreign discussants. It nearly exclusively handled foreign personalities and extras for the Japanese media since its inception in 1985, and it handled all of *KHN*'s discussants. While this simplified both payment and management, IMO did much more. It conducted the auditions and looked for foreign talent on the street.[4] Furthermore, contrary to the producer's stress on nonprofessional ordinariness, some discussants appeared in the media well before *KHN* aired. And it was those hidden talents that were purposely assigned to play key roles in heating up the debate on the program. A most infamous case in point was that of a Japanese American man who worked as disc jockey. With his suntanned face, he agitated the people in the studio by making offensive comments from the viewpoint of an American hard-liner. While audiences might not have been aware that this was a media-manipulating performance, other foreign discussants knew who the far from ordinary talents from IMO are. Some foreign discussants who passed the audition were very sensitive to and frustrated by those who made provocative comments in the producer's favor. I return to this point later. Suffice it to say here that the way the ordinariness of the discussants was highly stage-managed worked to marginalize some discussants' presence on the show.

MULTINATIONAL REPRESENTATION OF THE GLOBAL SOCIETY

The commodification of ordinary foreigners on *KHN* was suggestive of two reasons for the end of the West-centered *gaijin-tarento* on Japanese TV that was observed in the late 1990s. First was the substantial increase in foreign nationals who speak fluent Japanese. Second was the growing prominence of non-Western countries in the world and the increasing recognition that the Japanese people needed to refute foreigners' (improper) views of Japan (*Housou Bunka*, November 1996). These changes also needed to be grasped in conjunction with the paradigm shift from internationalism to globalism discussed in chapter 3. The phenomenon of *KHN* clearly showed the emphasis shift in terms of the collusive othering from the (imbalanced) internationalist binary between "Japan" and "the West" to that of the globalist binary between "Japan" and the "rest" of the world's nations. The rise of non-Western players in the global economy, politics, and culture, as well as an increase in communication and exchange among the non-Western nations that overpass Western countries, have urged Japanese media to pay more attention to non-Western countries and their perspectives and hence to shift the composition of *gaijin-tarento* on Japanese TV. This tendency was clearly demonstrated on *KHN*, in which the binary contraposition of "Japan" versus "the West" gave way to more representations of the global society. Many of the popular discussants (and performers) in *KHN* were actually from Asia and Africa, and their "non-Western" views were even more emphasized in the program.

Surely, the hitherto suppressed voices of Asian and African discussants might offer fresh insights into Japanese culture and society. They displayed critical views on Japanese racial discrimination from the perspective of the people concerned. Yet the program did not just aim to throw these insights into the limelight. No less important, underlining those voices was necessary to depict the global society in microcosm in terms of the contraposition of Japan and other nations. The producer consciously included foreign discussants from as many countries and regions as possible so that the program could pretend to represent the whole world, as demonstrated by the program's claim that it featured "foreign people from more than fifty nations" (*More*, July 1999). To emphasize the picture of Japan versus the world, the studio set was organized in such a way that foreign nationals and their Japanese counterparts stood face-to-face, and foreign discussants were required to wear the national flag of their countries on their chests. Furthermore, the production side regularly asked, if not compelled, foreign discussants to make comments based on comparisons between Japan and their own nations. The least favorable comment for the program for the producer was the one that stresses similarities between Japan and other nations. In my observation of the studio shooting, I heard some discussants complain that this black-and-white framework obscured the complexity of the issues concerned. Such views tended to be edited out, if they were successfully expressed at all, and the deviant discussant soon disappeared from the program.

The global diversity represented on the program is thus fundamentally a one-dimensional composition of a nationalized binarism that eliminates ambiguity and multiplicity in the form of national belonging and ethnocultural identity. Although some discussants obtained dual citizenship and some had lived in Japan since childhood, they were all categorized as "foreign-national residents." For example, one man wearing the South Korean flag was born in Japan and had lived in the United States, South Korea, and Japan, but he was categorized as a representative of South Korea. He was lumped together with other South Korea nationals, some of whom had come to Japan rather recently, and the national flag he put on all too easily reduced his opinions to Korean viewpoints. He insisted on his doubleness and "cosmopolitan identity" in his personal web page and expressed it in an interview in a Japanese-language magazine targeted at resident Koreans in Japan.[5] However, his doubleness was never attended to on the program. All he is expected to do is act unambiguously Korean.

This was reminiscent of a familiar problematic associated with multiculturalism. Multiculturalism was criticized for its underlying conception of culture as a coherent entity, which went together with the conception of a multicultural society as a mosaic composed of clearly demarcated boundaries between ethnic cultures with the dominant group unmarked as such. More recently, the idea of multiculturalism had also been blamed for failing to take transnationalism into consideration; its obsession with multicultural situations "here," in a national society, for the purpose of socionational integration often tended to disregard migrants' connections with "there," which is often regarded as a detriment to communal harmony in the multicultural nation (Vetrovec 2001).

It seemed premature to see the same multiculturalist trap in the Japanese context in which even the idea of multicultural coliving had not yet been well embraced by the government and the populace, not to mention the need to adopt related policies to advance multiculturalism. Rather the issue at stake with regard to the cultural politics of *KHN* was, I suggest, multinationalism. The program's representation of the global society rendered national belonging as even more taken for granted through the pleasurable consumption of a multinational spectacle. By suppressing foreign discussants' ambivalent (trans)national connections and sense of belonging to Japan, the program fixed them as foreign-national others, essentially cutting them off from Japan. It was an attempt to control the implosion of difference within an imagined community by replacing it with a multinational situation that consisted of a mob of temporary residents who will never be full members of the nation. They were allowed to express their difference in public only as long as they wore national flags that emphasized the division between "us" and "them." Their differences were recognized and understood exclusively as "in but not of" in the highly commodified form of national branding.

THE MEDIA SPECTACLE OF A "WAR OF WORDS" IN A GLOBAL ERA

The program format of a "war of words" (*zessen*) between Japanese and ordinary foreigners made *KHN*'s multinationalism work more effectively. This is related to the second reason for the end of the era of the *gaijin-tarento*. In the age of internationalism, *gaijin-tarento* pleasurably confirmed Japanese uniqueness to the Japanese people. However, thankfully accepting Western views on Japanese uniqueness was no longer satisfactory. As uniqueness had become associated less with the secret of Japan's economic power than with the shortcomings that account for its socioeconomic decline, and as actual encounters with foreign nationals were becoming uncommon in everyday settings, the need to refute the improper views, criticisms, and misunderstandings about Japan that are uttered by foreigners had come to be stressed. Reflecting this trend, *KHN* presented not just foreign people's anger and criticism against Japanese society but also Japanese counterarguments (in a highly emotional manner in most cases). Provocative statements about Japanese bizarreness by a foreign discussant were followed by a studio discussion between other foreign discussants, who commented on the statement from their own national perspectives, and Japanese discussants, who often got excited and further stirred up the quarrel. Extremely confrontational performances on both sides worked well together to excitingly demarcate ethnocultural boundaries between Japan and other nations.

This picture overlaps with a new type of *nihonjinron* appearing in the age of globalization. For example, Ishii Yoneo argued for the importance of acquiring "global literacy" in his book with Kawai Hayao, *The Japanese and Globalization* (2002). To acquire global literacy, the mastering of basic communications skills in English, as the global lingua franca, is indispensable first of all, but this is just a means to an end. From his own experience in promoting international exchanges between Japan and the rest of the world, Ishii pointed out that it is not an exchange but a one-way method of introducing Japanese culture to the world and vice versa. What is imperative in the age of globalization is, he argued, an international exchange that does not just sponsor superficial cultural exhibitions but promotes a discussion that might be highly antagonistic in some cases. In the face of increases in the clash of opinions, values, and principles among people of different national backgrounds, a passive attitude toward defending and protecting Japanese culture or convincing oneself that Japan will always be incomprehensible to others, Ishii argued, must be discarded. Japanese people have to learn to actively express their own opinions, to maintain Japan's positions and interests, and even to be prepared for serious confrontation with other nationals in the global arena.

Conforming to this view, the Japanese media often appreciated *KHN* in terms of the representation of Japanese discussants' head-on back talk to those foreigners who asserted their sense of anger and frustration with Japanese society without reserve. Their self-assertiveness could be seen as lopsided, but at the same time, their ability to express their own opinions in a foreign language in a public space was regarded as something Japanese people should emulate. No less entertaining to audiences was watching how Japanese people who were supposed to be unskilled at debate subtly refute such skillfully argumentative foreign discussants.[6] Watching *KHN*, Japanese audiences could release their pent-up emotions, which were heightened in the rather stifling Japanese socioeconomic situation under the rough waves of globalization, and enjoyed the spectacle of Japanese retorting to "ill-advised" foreigners in an exaggerated manner.

The nonfiction writer Hisada Megumi's comment that the program made her head go round (*Asahi Shinbun*, March 2, 1999, evening ed.) hit the mark in regard to how the Olympic-like war of words between Japanese and foreign discussants effectively distorted the public visibility and discussion of multicultural issues in the Japanese context. In watching *KHN*, she was overwhelmed by the diversity of nationalities of people residing in Japan and their assertion, in fluent Japanese, of the anger and frustration they are made to feel living in Japan, so much so that she could not help but realize that Japan had become a multiracial society without her knowledge. This suggests that the public visibility and utterances of foreign residents with competency in Japanese might urge Japanese audiences to turn their attention to how the intensified cross-border flows of people have made it untenable to believe in the homogeneity of the Japanese imagined community.

At the same time, however, Hisada also confessed that she was surprised to find a strong nationalistic sentiment evoked within her as she was annoyed by the foreigners' Japan-bashing and her inability to refute it. Here we can see how the multinational framework of the war of words operated to incite viewers' antagonistic reaction against growing cultural diversity within the society. Through TV's aptitude for entertaining simplification, such a chance was subtly replaced by the representation of a controllable confrontation of national-cultural diversity. The program reduced multicultural situations to a multinational spectacle by employing the framework of a global war of words between clearly demarcated nationalities whereby the potential to deconstruct the exclusive imagined communities from within were precluded and domesticated by the fortification of exclusive international diversity (Bhabha 1990).

THE CULTURAL POLITICS OF PUBLIC VISIBILITY

While multinationalism based on the distorted representation of multicultural situations in Japan should be critically examined, the fact that *KHN* made foreign-national residents visible and their hitherto suppressed voices audible in a mediated public space cannot be entirely dismissed. This point was suggestive of the argument concerning public participation in American talk shows such as *Oprah* in terms of the possibility of constructing plural public spheres. Those shows are often criticized for the vulgar quality of debate among the studio participants, but they are also appreciated for underlining repressed issues and providing a forum for the voices of women, working-class people, homosexuals, and ethnic minorities in the mainstream media. Paulo Carpignano and his collaborators, for example, thought highly of talk shows' role in democratizing the public sphere (Carpignano et al. 1990). By intensifying the confrontation between the persons concerned and studio audiences, they argued, American talk shows make it possible for the hitherto inaudible experience and voice of ordinary people to gain an advantage over intellectuals' pedagogical comments in the public sphere. Talk shows thus break through the limitation of a Habermasian bourgeois public sphere that is criticized for being elitist, male dominated, and racially exclusive in operation (Livingstone and Lent 1994).

Similarly, it could be argued that *KHN* contributed to making invisible foreign residents and their voices public matters. For example, many issues related to racial discrimination that had tended to be disregarded by Japanese TV were dealt with in the programs, if in an excessively sensational and superficial manner. Issues such as the bigoted comment of Ishihara Shintaro, the governor of Tokyo, that Chinese and Korean residents were associated with the increase in foreigners' crime and the discriminatory practices of a public bath in Otaru, Hokkaido, that forbade foreigners to enter it, were covered and critically discussed from the point of view of those who were discriminated against. In the latter case, two foreign discussants flew to Otaru to cover the story on the program of February 28, 2001.[7] Their coverage was mostly from the viewpoint of a Japanese American man who is married to a Japanese woman and has Japanese nationality but was forbidden to enter the bath due to his "foreign" appearance. He brought a suit against the bath owner in order to let the Japanese public know how this kind of conduct, which was still not uncommon in Japan, was seriously discriminatory and racist (Arudou 2003). In Japan, which lacks any penal regulations, a sign reading "no foreigners allowed" was openly posted at the door of some real estate agencies and bars. Yet such discrimination was, if pointed out at all in the media, rarely viewed as intolerable conduct. Following the journalistic principle of "objectivity and nonpartisan impartiality," the Japanese mass media tended to offer "balanced" coverage of such cases by hearing both sides of the story and pointing out the difficulty of multicultural coliving in a detached manner, ending with the clichéd suggestion that to maintain social harmony both sides should get together and discuss the issue.[8]

In *KHN*'s coverage, nearly all foreign discussants condemned the prohibition of those who have "foreign" appearance to enter a public bath as racial discrimination, supporting the standpoint of the persons concerned. This created an unusual opportunity for the voices of the discriminated people to be heard in the mainstream media, and so it should not be easily dismissed as too subjective and biased. Foregrounding the minority's point of view, the myth of media objectivity and neutrality that is actually inclined to work for maintaining the status quo was debunked. The fact that such objectivity was only beneficial to the majority of the Japanese populace is exposed.

This should not, let me reiterate, divert attention from the fact that talk shows are highly stage-managed and controlled by the production side. We need to interrogate how supposedly spontaneous voices on the show are actually shaped under the production format of the talk show genre and whether a highly commodified and exaggerated debate on TV can be seen as a public forum. As Jane Shattuc (1997) argued, professional masters of ceremonies are apt to dissociate the issue under discussion from a wider social context and reduce it to a personal matter to be resolved at the individual level. Despite the possibility of constructing an alternative public sphere, media gatekeepers' emphasis on sensationalism and personification deprives TV talk shows of a critical edge. Such criticism could be well-applied to *KHN*, whose degree of stage-management and preclusion of the potential for creating a multicultural public sphere were not comparable to its American counterparts.

Rather, the point I'd like to bring up here is the limitation of posing a Manichean question of whether audience-participation talk programs that foreground hitherto unenunciated voices of the marginalized create a new kind of public forum or are merely commodified TV spectacles. It would be more productive, I would argue, to analyze the multicultural politics of TV talk shows by acknowledging that these aspects cannot be considered separately but complement each other. Putting aside a bipolar view of spectacle or forum, circus or symposium, Joshua Gamson (1998) argued that, as they exist between two opposing poles, American talk shows blur the lines and redraw them at the same time. With a particular focus on the issue of homosexuality, Gamson empirically analyzed how boundaries between private and public and normal and abnormal are at once obscured and reconstructed by attending to the contradiction in the public appearance of marginalized people. Television talk shows highlight what he called "paradoxes of visibility," which display

> democratization through exploitation, truths wrapped in lies, normalization through freak show. There is in fact no choice here between manipulative spectacle and democratic forum, only the puzzle of a situation in which one cannot exist without the other, and the challenge of seeing clearly what this means for a society at war with its own sexual diversity. (Gamson 1998, 19)

In exploring the paradoxes, Gamson attached particular importance to the examination of how marginalized people actively participate and, in some instances, collude in this media event. While admitting the significance of the analysis of the way in which the media production and representation "annihilate" and "deform" gay and lesbian people, he nevertheless pointed out its limitations in analyzing talk shows by posing a question about their agencies in the process.

[W]hat happens to media representations of nonconforming sexualities when
lesbian and gay men are actively invited to participate, to "play themselves"
rather than be portrayed by others, to refute stereotypes rather than simply
watch them on the screen? That is the twist talk shows provide. (Gamson
1998, 22)

Gamson argued that public visibility through commercial media is something
like "walking a tight rope" for the marginalized people. They cannot control
the result of their public visibility though media entertainment shows, and
there is no guarantee that it would lead to the deconstruction of their negative
stereotypes. Nevertheless, "the struggle for self-representation is not one in
which talk show guests are simple victims. . . . [T]hey have a strong hand in
creating it" (Gamson 1998, 215). Critical analysis of how talk shows represented and exploited marginalized people in terms of the democratization of
the public sphere appeared to take the side of the marginalized. Yet there is a
risk that it eventually subsumes their active practices and performances of
becoming visible under a bigger picture of the construction of the rational
public sphere, a risk of disregarding the existing heterogeneous and contradictory practices of the marginalized within and behind the public sphere.

Likewise, I suggest that examining the active participation and performance of foreign discussants in *KHN* is imperative if we are to grasp the
complexity and ambivalence involved in the multinationalist attempt to re-
construct national boundaries through media entertainment. While its symbolic violence to boundary demarcation cannot be stressed too much, we
should also carefully look at various practices of the represented in the site of
production and consumption in order to go beyond an oversimplified picture.
This is not to uncritically celebrate the autonomy and active resistance of the
marginalized to the mass media. Increased attention to those aspects, since
they do not evidently appear on the surface of the mediated public sphere and
thus cannot be grasped by representational analysis, I argue, would lead to a
many-layered understanding of cultural politics and representational violence
on *KHN*. A detailed field research analysis of how heterogeneous foreign
discussants performed in various ways on the show was indispensable for
this purpose, yet it was beyond the scope of this chapter. In the remainder, I
offer some findings and considerations drawn from my limited field research.

PERFORMING "FOREIGNERS" AND THE
BURDEN OF REPRESENTATION

While it appears that foreign discussants tended to assert their differences in
a nationalistic and ethnocentric manner on the program, once we met those
discussants who behaved like nationalists on the screen it often became apparent that they were not nationalists at all. For example, a Chinese graduate

student strongly defended China's position on the show, but she was critical of Chinese society and the government in an interview with me. Admitting that she tended to become nationalistic on the show, she told me, "I am not quite sure why I'd be [nationalistic] in the studio discussion, but perhaps I enjoy behaving that way. It is more enjoyable on that occasion [than being a rational thinker]. It is something like participating in the Olympics." She thus fully followed the intention of the producer and enjoyed performing accordingly. Similarly a Japanese Brazilian journalist stated that while he tried not to be taken in, contrary to his initial intention, he often found himself behaving in a manner that supported the aim of the producer, strongly defending Brazil's position vis-à-vis Japan in response to Japanese discussants' comments. In either case, the program's organizing format of war of words also induced foreign discussants to feel "you have no right to say that to me and my country" and responded nationalistically. Here, too, we can see that multinationalism effectively worked to generate the self-assertion of one's belonging to a particular nation.

However, foreign discussants' seemingly nationalistic performances were not just colored by their (often pleasurable) participation in the media show. They could also be seen as reflecting the burden of representation caused by their position as a marginalized citizen in Japan. Most foreign discussants applied for the audition of their own accord, and there were many practical reasons for their eagerness to participate. Some wanted to earn extra pocket money, some wanted to take advantage of their TV appearances to acquire better jobs in Japan, and some even wanted to become media celebrities. But there were also those who were motivated to contest widely held negative stereotypes of the country with which they (fully or partially) identified because such images strongly affected their identity formation and living conditions within Japan. Those from Asia and Africa, who, unlike people of Western origin, suffered much more severe prejudice and discrimination in Japan, were particularly apt to work hard to improve the images of their own countries. As the Chinese discussant mentioned above noted:

> I'd strongly argue against any criticism of Chinese society and culture on the show. Well, of course I know there are so many bad things in China that need to be reformed and changed. But that is another story. We do not have to show such bad aspects of China on Japanese TV. I'd rather wipe them out.

I was also informed that some Japanese Brazilian participants deliberately referred to the positive sides of Brazil as much as possible in order to tear down unjustly spread images of their backwardness. And some participants from African countries took an opposite tack and enhanced their images by representing a poor but "pure" Africa on the show. In this sense, even if they seemed to be behaving like nationalists, they did so for strategic reasons.

This kind of performance was sometimes forced on participants by their expatriate communities in Japan. For example, the Chinese participant told me that there was strong peer pressure on Chinese discussants to make pro-China comments on the program. And if they did not meet this expectation, their peers often condemned them. According to the Chinese woman, intense discussion occurred over several months concerning the comments made by Chinese participants on *KHN* in the readers' column of a Chinese-language newspaper published in Japan. It became the focus of criticism, as it was perceived to be damaging to the image of China and Chinese in Japan. My informant was the subject of much criticism over her failure to enhance the image of China. "If I could not respond well to the criticism made against China or could not well defend China's position on the show," she said, "I was blamed for my unsatisfactory performance by the people around me."

The case of a participant from Iran was more serious. An unknown Iranian man suddenly hit the participant in the face as he entered his favorite bar in Roppongi, where many foreign nationals gathered for a drink. The person was angry over his performance on the show and the way he described Iran. He accused my informant of strengthening the negative images of Iranians in Japan. In both cases, the burden of representation put pressure on the foreign discussants followed the multinationalistic strategy of the program.

In any case, participants only had control of their representation during the off-air taping of the program. Even if they had the opportunity to give their comments in the studio, there was no guarantee that the scenes would be broadcast. Shooting the program usually took more than three hours while the broadcast was around forty-five minutes, including the video coverage. Most of the discussion was cut in the postproduction process. It was in this regard, as mentioned earlier, that the presence of IMO talents on the show highly frustrated other participants. Their more frequent appearance in the program was perceived as unfair not simply because they collaborated with the producer but because the performance of their assigned roles on the show was thought to guarantee their frequent on-screen time. One participant expressed his sense of discontent that they were not really qualified to participate in the program.

> Their views of Japan are fundamentally different from ours. Their views of Japan are actually those of insiders, as they have been mostly brought up in Japan. I think this makes it difficult for them to see Japan "objectively" from outside. They are awkward, halfway foreigners, as it were. They just pretend [to be foreigners].

The sense of unfairness was also expressed in terms of language skills. Talk shows demand an instantaneous response with rhetorical sophistication, but those whose first language is not Japanese and who have not lived in Japan for long could not easily do this. As my informant told me, "I often feel vexed since we cannot compete with pseudo-foreigners in terms of discussion skills." Native language skills were also regarded as a sign of the lack of "foreignness."

Needless to say, it is questionable whether these views about "pseudo-foreigners" were qualified and whether it was at all possible to distinguish the "real" view of foreigners from a false one expressed on a TV talk show. It might be the case that those who were mostly brought up in Japan and spoke Japanese like a native also experienced a strong sense of frustration since they were nevertheless treated as second-class citizens in Japan. At the least the above comments show how foreign discussants were sensitive to the way in which the commodification of ordinary foreigners in the TV production actually worked to marginalize their presence and visibility on the show. And it should be considered a negative effect of this commodification that the heterogeneous voices and experiences of people who were categorized as foreigner in Japan were expressed in terms of an antagonistically demarcated boundary between authentic and unauthentic foreigners.

Moreover, the prevalence of some talent participants on the show pressured the other participants, overtly or covertly, to behave in accordance with the intentions of the producer to increase their on-air time.

> I try not to be a strong nationalist but often end up being like that. It is partly because the staff urges us to be so. You know, we do not want our comments to be cut, so we sometimes try to utter what will interest TV producers. Yes, we are conscious of the producers' intentions, so we perform accordingly.

As this comment indicates, participants' collusion in a multinational spectacle was actually a necessary measure taken to maximize their visibility on the show. Such performances by foreign discussants tended to reproduce the demarcation of national-cultural boundaries as they highlighted the image of ethnocentric foreigners who did not see the beam in their own eyes and simply attacked Japan. In this sense, it can be argued that their "walking the tight rope" was highly precarious. Nevertheless, unless they got on the rope, they did not even have the chance to fall down, and no matter how much they were conscious of the danger associated with public visibility many still wanted to get on the wire. This precariousness was the price that foreign residents had to, and perhaps were willing to, pay for going public through *KHN*.

The desire to be visible, recognized, and heard in the public sphere was quite strong and serious for some marginalized people (Gamson 1998). In the case of *KHN*, I found that, regardless of different personal motivations to join the program, most participants were keen to go public and have their say about Japan on a nationally networked TV program. It also gave them great pleasure to share the issues and problems they encountered in everyday life with those in similar circumstances. With this in mind, some, if not all, were determined to take on this risky business. As one participant told me:

> My friends often ask me why I am participating in a vulgar show like *KHN*, as this demeans me in public. . . . Well, I fully understand his comment. Nor do I think that participation in the program will make it easier to rent an apartment, to change the mind of the owner who turns us away at the door. I am not that naive. I know I am, after all, a foreigner here, even if I am a Japanese Brazilian. . . . But the studio is the only public space where we can complain [about Japan] and our say will be listened to. It is an exceptional occasion in a monotonous daily life. As we are always regarded as just foreigners no matter how long we have lived in Japan, our sense of resignation is so high. Yet those who participate in the show do not resign themselves to the current situation, with a will to change the situation, to change Japanese society.

This comment urges us to realize how program participation was significant in satisfying, if just partly, some foreign residents' strong desire to go public and how the symbolic violence affected by the TV industry, which distorted and exploited such desires, is rough. This is the power-infused ambivalence we need to consider in order to fully engage with the cultural politics of multinationalism on *KHN*.

RAISON D'ÊTRE OF "FOREIGNER" FOR JAPAN

Yet, let us be reminded that even such a humble desire for public visibility is at the mercy of the mass media. It is easily shut down due to the commercial logic that dominates the media industries. In March 2002, *KHN* went off the air. It reassured its audience that it would be back soon. A few special programs were broadcast, but nothing has happened since. As is the rule in the TV world, a drop in ratings is detrimental to the life of a program. Three and half years is not a short period for a weekly variety show, and the producer would say that *KHN* had exhausted its potential. This may be true for commercial purposes. But it is not true for the Japanese media, which have not yet fulfilled their duty for creating a more egalitarian and inclusive public sphere.

The Japanese media's report on the crimes committed by someone who looks like a "foreigner" continues. Alternatively, foreign-national residents are featured in the media to play the role of assuring the international appeal of Japanese cultures. A prominent example is the TV program *Cool Japan* that has been produced by a semi-public broadcasting company, NHK's satellite channel, since 2006. The program aims to revisit various Japanese cultures to find hitherto unnoticed attractiveness that is to be globally appreciated through the eyes of foreign-national residents. This is clearly in line with the escalating interests in nation branding and the Cool Japan promotion policy. What is still missing is any aspiration for the mass media to recognize foreign nationals as citizens of Japanese society, not as useful foreigners for an exclusive demarcation of national-cultural borders of Japan.

NOTES

1. There were some nonwhite stars, such as Osmond Sanko from West Africa, whose performance of "primitiveness" and funny "Africanness" were much enjoyed by Japanese audiences. For the representation of black people in the Japanese mass media, see Russel (1991). Yet no person of Asian descent emerged as a TV celebrity. Marginalized groups such as resident Koreans have been treated as taboo on Japanese TV programs until recently.

2. This chapter analyzes *KHN* with a focus on the drawing of boundaries between Japan and the foreign, but the cultural politics of its representation is by no means restricted to this. Particularly in its latter stages, perhaps to overcome the mannerisms of the content, the role of foreign discussants changed. Most commonly, the program foregrounds such queer and bizarre Japanese as motorcycle gangs, homosexuals, overweight people, and high school women in the sexual trades (*enjo-kousai*). Foreign discussants play the role of taking a stand against them. The foreign discussants' comments are sensationally represented as a substitution for the conservative views against the marginalized that are assumed to be held by the majority of Japanese audiences so that the program can be subtly acquitted of the charge of showcasing degrading views by using foreigners' gazes as a safe filter. For the gender politics of *KHN*, see Hagiwara (2003) and Kunihiro (2003).

3. My field research was conducted in Tokyo between May 2000 and November 2001. In addition to the interview with the producer, I observed the program being shot in the studio and conducted informal interviews with some of the foreign discussants.

4. Television production companies and talent offices play a significant role in choosing "appealing amateurs" for audience-participation programs. See *Nikkei Trendy*, March 2003, 154–55.

5. See *Senuri*, no. 51 (2002).

6. See, for example, *Sapio*, March 10, 1999, 96–97.

7. In the latter period of the show, some discussants were assigned video coverage of the issue of the week, and the film was shown in the studio for discussion.

8. See, for example, *NHK News 11*, February 9, 1999.

Chapter Five

The Korean Wave and the Dis/empowering of Resident Koreans in Japan

East Asian media flows and connections have been evolving since the mid-1990s. In this development, Japanese media culture took the initiative, but with the rise of other East Asian media cultures, the flows are becoming more and more multilateral. Most notably, in the twenty-first century, South Korean media culture is sweeping over Asian markets, a phenomenon called "Korean Wave." South Korean TV dramas and pop music are receiving a warmer welcome in places like Taiwan, Hong Kong, and China than their Japanese equivalents. Japan, too, is embracing the Korean Wave. While local channels such as Fukuoka TVQ began to broadcast South Korean TV drama series as early as 1996, it is especially around the end of the 1990s that South Korean films and TV dramas came to be well received in Japan. As far as TV dramas are concerned, in 2002, the national-network channel TV Asahi broadcast for the first time *All about Eve* at prime time. The series was not successful in terms of ratings, but it opened the door for the entry of South Korean TV dramas into the major media space in Japan. However, it was not until *Winter Sonata* was phenomenally popular in 2003 that the landing of the Korean Wave in the Japanese market was clearly marked, which has been hitherto exclusive to other Asian TV dramas. Since then, various TV dramas and popular music from South Korea have attracted a huge number of audiences in Japan.

This chapter examines the complexity of the impact of the Korean Wave on Japanese society and considers the possibility of transnational dialogues through media and cultural connections by taking the popularity of *Winter Sonata* as a case in point. A comparison of the reception of *Winter Sonata* in

particular with the fervent reception of Hong Kong media culture in the late
1990s shows how the nostalgia perceived by consuming South Korean TV
dramas has more to do with personal sentiments and memories, and this leads
to more self-reflective post-text activities such as learning the Korean language, visiting South Korea, and even studying the history of Japanese colonialism. However, there is another crucial difference between the reception
of Hong Kong and South Korean media culture. It is the existence of postcolonial subjects within Japan. To understand the complexity of transnational
media connections promoted by the Korean Wave, I argue, it is also crucial
to consider how the media flows from South Korea have influenced, both
constructively and unconstructively, the social positioning and recognition of
resident Koreans in Japan, most of whom are the descendants of expatriates
under Japanese colonial rule. I consider this by examining the representation
of and audience responses to a popular Japanese TV drama series that, for the
first time, deals with sociohistorical issues about resident Koreans in prime
time. It will be suggested that while the social recognition of resident Koreans has been much improved as the Korean Wave significantly betters the
image of South Korea, it tends to disregard the understanding of historically
embedded experiences of resident Koreans. They are instead effortlessly
associated with the culture and people of South Korea in a way in which
postcolonial and multicultural issues are subsumed under inter-nationalized
understanding of cross-border cultural connections and exchange.

NOSTALGIA AND SELF-REFLEXIVITY

The Korean Wave is not the first instance where other Asian media texts
have been well received in the Japanese market. Various kinds of films
(mostly of Hong Kong) and stars such as Bruce Lee, Jackie Chan, and Dick
Lee have been favorably received as they appealingly represent different
kinds of cultural expressions and imaginations in Asia. Most recently, there
was a Hong Kong boom in the late 1990s, which is still fresh in our memories.[1] A comparison of the reception of Hong Kong media culture in the late
1990s and that of the Korean Wave in the early twenty-first century eluci-
dates both similarities and differences between them in intriguing ways.

First of all, the scope and intensity of media and cultural flows from
South Korea is not comparable to those from other Asian regions and countries. In particular, the passionate reception of *Winter Sonata* reached an
unprecedented level. The Hong Kong boom was promoted by women's magazines and film and music industries; it did not attract much attention from
most of the mainstream media, especially TV. Extra efforts were thus needed
for audiences to watch videos and get information about the stars, and they
faced difficulties in sharing their interests in Hong Kong media culture with

friends and colleagues. Accordingly, the Hong Kong boom's audiences were relatively limited to devoted fan communities. Yet, precisely because of this, many fans were proud to have an "advanced" taste, which enabled them to differentiate themselves from mass consumers of the mainstream media culture in Japan. It is also crucial here to remember that Hong Kong TV dramas have never been shown in the mainstream, free-to-air TV channels in Japan, but TV dramas as well as films are the main vehicles of the Korean Wave and thus terrestrial national channels, which are the most influential media in Japan, are main promoters of the boom. Notably, *Winter Sonata* was broadcast on NHK, a public TV channel, which has the most extensive penetration all over the country. In addition, various kinds of mass media, such as newspapers and magazines, regularly cover the story about the drama, actors, and audience responses.

The Hong Kong boom and Korean Wave have something in common as well in that the well-received media texts represent modern cultural scenes in urban settings. While sharing the experience of negotiating with American (and, perhaps to a lesser extent, Japanese) influences of production styles, Hong Kong and South Korean media industries have developed their own styles of films, pop music, and youth-oriented dramas that attain transnational appeal in terms of the representation of "here and now" in Asian urban contexts. They lucidly articulate the intertwined composition of global homogenization and heterogenization in a different way from those of Japanese media texts.

It can be argued, however, that one of the main reasons for the success of South Korean TV dramas is that, unlike their Hong Kong counterparts, their depiction of family matters and relationships enable them to appeal to a wider range of viewers than Japanese programs. Even for young viewers in East Asia, South Korean dramas are preferable to Japanese ones in terms of realism and their ability to relate to the characters and story lines. In my interviews with Taiwanese university students in 2001, I was told that Japanese series tend to focus solely on young people's loves and jobs, and this restricts the scope of their stories and thus audience identification. South Korean dramas, on the other hand, while featuring young people's romances as a central theme, tend to portray the problems and bonds of parents and children, grandparents, and other relatives. This makes them look more similar to the actual lives of young people living in Taiwan. The restricted and closed relationships and daily lives of young people featured in the world of Japanese TV dramas, which Mamoru Ito (2004) describes as a "microcosm," have attracted many followers in the Asian region. While South Korean TV drama production might have been influenced by this kind of Japanese drama production (Lee 2004), South Korean dramas have achieved a different kind of realism in portraying East Asian urban imaginaries.

However, this does not fully account for the favored reception of *Winter Sonata* in Japan. It is rather the sense of nostalgia that marks its adoring reception. This shows another similarity to the reception of Hong Kong and South Korean media texts in that the main audiences are women in their thirties to sixties who tend to express their nostalgic feelings for the things that used to be in Japan in their reception of Hong Kong and South Korean media texts. In the case of Hong Kong culture, it reminded Japanese audiences of the vigor of the society that supposedly has been lost in Japan. This sense of nostalgia was strongly contextualized in the situation in which Japan struggled with an economic slump after the collapse of the so-called bubble economy while other Asian nations enjoyed high economic growth beginning in the early 1990s. In this suffocating socioeconomic atmosphere, Japanese audiences' consumption of Hong Kong media culture was sharply marked by a nostalgic longing for lost social vigor. This mode of reception shows a highly ambivalent posture in the appreciation of cultural neighbors. An awareness of "familiar" cultural differences through the consumption of Hong Kong media culture arouses contrasting senses, a sense that Hong Kong's level of being modern still lags behind Japan, albeit only slightly, and a sense of contemporaneity in living in the same temporality that promotes cultural dialogue on equal terms. On the one hand, Japanese audiences' emphasis on the temporal difference rather than the spatial one occasionally displays their failure and refusal to see other Asians as modern equals who share exactly the same developmental temporality. This might attest to a historically constituted Japan's double claim for being similar but superior to "Asia." Orientalist thinking that attempts to understand Asia's present by equating it with Japan's past good times occasionally resurfaces in the nostalgic appreciation of Hong Kong culture (Iwabuchi 2002a).

On the other hand, however, it also shows Japanese audiences' appreciation of a different mode of Asian modernity on more than equal terms with Japan in terms of negotiation with the West and the sophistication of cultural hybridization. Hong Kong's present was appreciated as a promising vivacity of another Asian modernity that was in stark contrast to Japan's present. By realizing that Hong Kong is no less developed and modernized than Japan and by positively identifying themselves with its sophisticated media texts, Japanese female audiences tried to regain vigor and energy themselves (Iwabuchi 2002a). This perception may prove to be an opportune moment for Japanese people to critically review the state of their own modernity. Belief in Japan's superiority over the rest of Asia—a condescending mode of thinking that, while accepting that the country belongs geographically and culturally to Asia, makes a distinction between Japan and Asia—remains firmly rooted in society, but such attitudes are being shaken as countries in Asia become more and more interconnected through media and cultural flows.

The same is true with the reception of *Winter Sonata* in Japan, as a news reporter from South Korea pointed out: "Cultures of other Asian countries evoke, touch and revive the emotions and dreams that have been lost in one country. This is a wonderful gift of cultural diversity" (*Asahi Shinbun*, May 18, 2004). Furthermore, revived emotions induce self-reflexive attitudes in audiences and drive them to search for a better present. However, nostalgia projected on to the South Korean TV drama *Winter Sonata* is slightly yet significantly different. While both nostalgias are sociohistorically structured and self-reflexive, in Hong Kong's case, nostalgia is projected more on to a societal loss perceived as such by individuals, but in the case of *Winter Sonata*, it is projected less on to the social vigor Japan allegedly has lost than on to personal memories and sentiments in terms of emotions of love and interpersonal relationships. This causes a crucial difference in the perception of coevalness (see Fabian 1983). In contrast to a highly precarious way of interpreting the cultural difference of Hong Kong in a temporal framework, the reception of *Winter Sonata* and other South Korean TV dramas in general seems to escape this pitfall. Actually, such a condescending view is more often than not found in the media discourse about the phenomenon, which aims to dismiss South Korean TV dramas as the belated equivalent of Japanese dramas in the 1960s and 1970s and to mock dissatisfied middle-aged female audiences who find a savior in South Korean TV dramas that actually reflect the behind-the-time standing of the society. This is mostly evident in men's weekly magazines, while the depiction is more sympathetic to the experiences of audiences in those magazines whose target readers are women and whose articles are predominately written by women.

It can be argued that Japanese audiences of *Winter Sonata* also perceive a temporal gap, given that most audiences are older women compared to their South Korean counterparts. Those middle-aged women are reminded of the pure passion for love and caring in human relationships that, according to them, they used to have in their youth. However, I found that the audiences do not seem to associate the temporal gap to that between the two societies even if they compare *Winter Sonata* with Japanese dramas of the 1970s and 1980s, precisely due to the fact that the longing for things that used to be is induced more at the level of personal memories and love sentiments rather than at the level of social loss. If, in the Hong Kong case, the sense of nostalgia is closely related to the discourse of vanishing (Ivy 1995), discourses about social loss in the course of modernization, in the South Korean case it has more to do with the personal recovery of vanished sentiments. And this longing is also related to the vanishing of discourse, the failure of Japanese media industries to produce media narratives that inspire emotions in a positive and humane manner. Most obviously, it is a pure, single-minded, loving, affectionate, and sympathetic interpersonal relationship depicted in *Winter Sonata* that attracts Japanese audiences. Especially admired is the man's magnanimous tenderness that subtly combines embracing leadership and sincere respect for his partner that is attractively performed by Bae Yon-jung. This is something that cannot be found in Japanese TV dramas, and one producer acknowledged that Japanese TV producers would not be able to make such dramas since such pure love stories have been replaced by stories with more ironic twists (*Asahi Shinbun*, May 21, 2004).

Interestingly, the highly personalized longing provoked by the reception of the South Korean drama has strong marks on the vivacity of post-text social praxis, which is crucially different from the Hong Kong case. Many audiences told me that they consciously tried to become more caring and gentle to others and respect family members after watching *Winter Sonata*. More significantly, compared to Hong Kong's case, in which many audiences tended to consciously indulge in the act of consuming media images and did not pay much interest in directly connecting with the people and culture of Hong Kong, audiences of *Winter Sonata* are much more actively making contact with South Korean culture, society, and people. Fascination evoked in the media texts more directly and actively leads to interest in knowing and encountering the "real" South Korea. No small number of people joins *Winter Sonata* tours to South Korea in order to experience the drama scenes, experience local culture and people, and start learning the language (Hirata 2008). Furthermore, many audiences are learning the history of Japanese colonialism in Korea. The nostalgic longing evoked by *Winter Sonata* is less motivated by the will to identify with the modernizing energy of the society, but precisely because of this personal-oriented desire, it is more engaging and emancipatory. Personal is indeed political!

INTER-NATIONAL CULTURAL EXCHANGE AND BEYOND

The historical relationship is also an important factor in understanding the development of the Korean Wave in Japan and its difference from its Hong Kong counterpart. Particularly important here is the history of Japan's colonialism, which has long rendered the relationship between the two countries geographically and culturally close yet politically and emotionally distant. The recent upsurge of the Korean Wave in Japan, which is based on the contemporaneous appreciation of its cultural neighbor, can be seen as a kind of positive reaction to the postwar closure of bilateral cultural exchange. Japan did have a history of imperial invasion to Hong Kong too. No small number of people in Hong Kong hold a strong anti-Japan sentiment, as is clearly shown by the demonstrations over the dispute about the possession of the *senkaku* islands. The point is, however, how the (post)colonial historical relationship is perceived and discussed in Japan. It is not a historical fact but the public perception of history and postcolonial presence that is at stake in the consideration of the way in which the history of Japanese colonialism inscribes the manner of Japanese reception of other Asian cultures. Japan's colonial relationship with Hong Kong has never been a big public issue in Japan—this is not to say it is insignificant—but the fact that South Korea is a former Japanese colony and no small number of people in South Korea have a strong antagonism toward Japan has long been widely recognized in Japan.

The bilateral relationship between Japan and South Korea has significantly improved since the late 1990s. The Seoul Olympics in 1988 was perhaps the first instance that changed Japanese images of South Korea from a backward, still-undeveloped country to an urbanized, modern country. The event attracted many tourists from Japan and activated grassroots exchange among the populaces. More significantly, two momentous events in the late 1990s greatly improved the cultural relationship between Japan and South Korea. One was the South Korean government's decision in late 1998 to abolish the long-term regulation policy of banning the import of Japanese culture. This announcement clearly signified a new epoch for the bilateral relationship and was particularly welcomed in Japan, since it seemed to mark the sign of historical reconciliation, at least on the part of the ex-colonizer.

As discussed in chapter 2, the Japanese government has been interested in the potential of media culture facilitating international exchange, particularly in terms of its capacity to improve Japan's reputation and to smooth Japan's historical reconciliation with other East and Southeast Asian countries. Cultural diplomacy in Asia has been implemented by the governmental circle at least since the 1970s, but it is mostly targeted toward Southeast Asia. Northeast Asia, especially Korea and China, whose colonial relationship with Japan is more direct and harsh but has not been seriously faced by the Japanese government since 1945, did not quite fit the scheme of cultural diplomacy until the late 1990s. Therefore, the recent development of media and cultural exchange between Japan and South Korea was widely perceived as a great advancement.

It is in this context that the concert of a Japanese duo, Chage and Aska, in Seoul in 2000 attracted massive media coverage in Japan. The duo had been actively entering other Asian markets. They had staged concerts in Taipei, Singapore, Hong Kong, Beijing, and Shanghai since 1994 but could not make it to South Korea due to the cultural regulation policy. Their inroads into East Asian markets might have been motivated by commercial reasons, but they are quite conscious of their role in overcoming Japanese imperial history. In August 2000, Chage and Aska finally held a concert in Seoul. The Japanese media enthusiastically covered it, reporting that this was a historic concert being the first performance by Japanese pop musicians in the Japanese language, which clearly marked a cultural thaw between Japan and South Korea. Chage and Aska expressed a sense of accomplishment at the concert: "Let us younger generations make a future together!" (*Asahi Shinbun*, August 28, 2000).

Yet what has become prominent is not just the entry of Japanese media culture into South Korea but, to an even greater degree, the advent of South Korean media culture into Japan. The two-way flow of media culture has significantly contributed to the people mutually finding intimate human faces and the immediate attractiveness of cultural neighbors. International exchange between Japan and South Korea was also greatly enhanced by the other historic event, the cohosting of the FIFA world cup soccer tournament. In 1996, to everyone's surprise, South Korea and Japan were assigned to cohost the FIFA soccer world cup in 2002. The two countries competed harshly with each other to win the bid and thus were not quite happy with the decision. However, the cohosting process eventually resulted in a tremendous impact on the betterment of the cultural relationship between the two nations at the official level as well as the grassroots level. It engendered many government-sponsored events, media collaborations such as the coproduction of TV dramas, and various kinds of people's cultural exchanges. When South Korea proceeded to the semifinal, people from Japan and South Korea, including resident Koreans, all gathered together to cheer South Korea in Shin-Okubo, a renowned Korean town in Tokyo.

Supporting this trend, some surveys showed the drastic improvement of people's mutual perceptions and a positive view about the future relationship between Japan and South Korea, with Japanese responses apparently being more positive. Likewise, many audiences of *Winter Sonata* expressed that the drama had totally changed their images of South Korean society, culture, and people, which were hitherto negative. By experiencing South Korea through post-text activities, they came to further realize the close ties the two countries have and the fallacy of Orientalist images of South Korea that have been dominantly held in Japanese society. According to a survey, about 60 percent of audiences came to have a better image of South Korea and 40 percent of audiences came to pay more attention to the media coverage of the Japan-Korea political and historical relationship (Hayashi 2004). It can be argued that this development is just a transient boom, and whether media consumption of *Winter Sonata* will lead to a substantial understanding of South Korea is doubtful. However, the change cannot be easily dismissed. In the post-text activities that characterize the *Winter Sonata* syndrome, some people even begin learning what Japanese colonialism did in the Korean peninsula and realize how it still casts a shadow on the countries' current situation. It probably will not lead to drastic political change in the short term, but the imagination and practice in everyday life is the basis of societal constitution. Through such mundane change, audiences will become active political agents (Mori 2008).

Having said this, admittedly caution is needed with regard to uncritical celebration for the role of media culture in the enhancement of international relationships. Being concerned mostly with the relationships between nations, such discussion tends to be put in the foreground by not attending to the complexity of transnational media and cultural flows and to redemarcate the national boundaries and disregard, and even suppress, the issues of existing differences, marginalization, and inequality within each society in terms of gender, sexuality, ethnicity, race, class, age, region, and so on. If we take cross-border dialogue engendered by media and cultural flows seriously, we must consider how the transnational circulations in media culture crisscross local multicultural and postcolonial issues. Then, if we are to take the Korean Wave in Japan seriously, an examination of how the Korean Wave has impacted the inter-national relationship between Japan and South Korea is not enough. An examination of its impact, I suggest, on the social positioning of resident Koreans in Japan who have long been discriminated against as second-rate citizens would be a significant touchstone in the consideration of the (im)possibility of mediated cross-border cultural dialogue.

KOREAN WAVE AND THE RECOGNITION
OF RESIDENT KOREANS

Resident Koreans are those who migrated to Japan during Japan's colonial rule and their descents. At the time of the end of World War II, roughly 2 million Koreans lived in Japan as Japanese nationals under colonial rule. More than 1.3 million people returned to Korea after the war, but about 60,000 Korans remained in Japan due to the difficulty of starting a new life and finding a job in Korea. Most of those remaining in Japan were the earliest migrants, who had firmly established their families in Japan and lost a substantial connection with Korea. Through the implementation of the San Francisco Peace Treaty in 1952, the Japanese government one-sidedly deprived those Koreans who had stayed in Japan of Japanese nationality and subjected them to the rigid control of the Alien Registration Law. Koreans then had two options other than remaining stateless residents in Japan; either return to Korea or naturalize to Japanese, but neither option was persuasive to many, though some Koreans repatriated to North Korean after 1959, responding to Kim Il Sung's encouragement of repatriation. The start of the diplomatic relationship between Japan and South Korea in 1965 made it possible for Koreans in Japan to obtain permanent residency if they became South Korean nationals. Still those who supported and identified themselves with North Korea remained stateless, neither Japanese nor South Korean. In either case, as a non-Japanese national, resident Koreans had to be registered as a foreigners living in Japan and used to carry a registration card, which included fingerprints until 1991 when their status as special permanent residents was fully acknowledged by the Japanese government. [2]

Some might wonder why many Koreans did not naturalize to Japanese despite the fact that they eventually lived in Japan for good. It is mostly due to the lingering structural discrimination against resident Koreans and the Japanese government's authoritarian immigration policy in order to keep the nation apparently "homogeneous." In the naturalization application procedure, resident Koreans experience a long, inhumane examination about the qualifications of becoming "properly Japanese," and are eventually required to adopt a Japanese name. Due to this strong assimilation policy, in order to become a Japanese citizen, Koreans are required to forget and hide their descent. Thus, no small number of them chooses not to become Japanese citizens, and this posture has been an important part of their identity formation in the resistance against the repression of the Japanese government. "Residing in Japan" (*zainichi*) is "an alternative to becoming naturalized," and the construction of their identity is centered on the sense of belongingness to Korean nations (Tai 2004, 356), while the number of Koreans who naturalize to Japanese has been increasing recently.

When we consider the impact of the Korean Wave in Japan, as suggested above, the presence of resident Koreans as (post)colonial subjects in Japan is decisively different from the Hong Kong case. The issue at stake here is whether and how the presence of problematic (post)colonial subjects has some bearing on the reception of media culture from the country in which they have ethno-historical "roots and routes" and/or how the reception has had an impact on local multicultural and postcolonial issues.

Ashley Carruthers (2004), in his analysis of the Japanese consumption of Vietnam exotic culture, argues that while it is a subjectless multiculturalism that tries to pleasurably domesticate multicultural situations in a highly consumerist manner without seriously engaging with the presence of actual subjects, what marks the Japanese case is a striking tendency that exotic Vietnamese cultures are introduced, exhibited, and promoted by Japanese people themselves. Here, the relative absence of Vietnamese residents in the Japanese public sphere as a significant other makes it much easier for people in Japan to consume Vietnamese culture as exotic:

> I wish to argue that there is another factor crucial to any understanding of the exceptional commodifiability of the Vietnamese exotic in Japan: the fact that the Vietnamese are not significant national others. . . . Vietmameseness in Japan is not embodied in a threatening way. It can be safely conceptualized in the abstract, untroubled by the prospect of encountering the concrete "ethnic" subject and its strange cooking smells and noisy music. (Carruthers 2004, 415–16)

Perhaps this point is applicable to the reception of Hong Kong culture, too. The relative absence of Hong Kong subjects in the public sphere renders the consumption of Hong Kong culture idealized and commodified.

Yet, as Carruthers (2004, 416) points out, this is never the case with South Korean culture: "The commodification of Koreanness is disrupted by a general distaste for the national otherness represented by diasporic or hybrid Korean identities." Resident Koreans have long been forced to live as a second-rate citizens in Japan and suffered considerable discrimination and prejudice, and many of them have been forced to live by passing as Japanese, hiding their ethnic backgrounds and adopting Japanese names in public. Koreanness is not something that can be comfortably consumed as a mass exotic commodity in the Japanese public imaginary unless its origin is suppressed or "Japanized," as is often the case with celebrities who willingly or unwillingly conceal their ethnic descents in public. Resident Koreans' cultural expressions have occasionally gained social recognition, as shown by several writers winning prizes for their novels, but they are not for pleasurable mass consumption. "Impure" identity construction that is neither Japanese nor Korean in a full sense has been a serious issue for them. Their cultural expressions thus tend to deal with the agony and ambiguity about their own precarious lives in the social positioning as *zainichi* who are historically torn between Japan and the Korean peninsula. And this in turn evokes something uneasy for Japan since its postcolonial subjectivity never allows it to cheerfully forget the history of colonialism.

In this context, the advent of the Korean Wave and the improvement of the images of South Korea in general pose intriguing questions about its relations to the social positioning and recognition of resident Koreans. As Charles Taylor (1994) argues, social recognition of difference is a significant aspect of the multicultural politics of the marginalized. Then the question is how are resident Koreans whose otherness cannot be easily contained by subjectless multiculturalism recognized via the fetishization of South Korean media culture? Does the recognition work to empower or disempower resident Koreans? How are positive perceptions of South Korea through the Korean Wave related to the perception of resident Koreans in Japan? How is their untamable postcolonial subjectivity, which resists easy cultural consumption, repositioned within Japan through the positive consumption of South Korean media culture and the advance of bilateral cultural exchange?

Of course, it depends. There are no straightforward answers to these questions, nor can we generalize the diverse experiences of resident Koreans. It cannot be denied that the rise of the Korean Wave and the betterment of South Korean images in Japan have significantly improved the images of resident Koreans, and this has empowered no small number of them. Some, especially the younger generations, have gained the confidence to live as Koreans in Japanese society without naturalizing to Japanese. Others have become more willing to bridge the two countries by positively taking advantage of his or her impure existence through activities that introduce various cultures to each other, such as film and popular music. The presence and issues about resident Koreans have come to be more frequently dealt with and attract more attention in the public media space, such as in popular magazines and TV shows. While *All Under the Moon* (1993) is the first commercially successful film about resident Koreans in Japan (see Iwabuchi 2000), recent films such as *GO* (2000) and *Pacchigi* (2005) are even better received.

At the same time, the impact of the Korean Wave still tends to be constrained by the dominant attention paid to international relationships, which overpowers the concern with resident Koreans. A sense of frustration is often expressed by resident Koreans in that Japanese people might embrace the Korean Wave, but the structure of social discrimination and indifference has not changed. For many resident Koreans, job opportunities are still limited, and it is at times not straightforward to rent a room. The improvement of these situations has not concerned the Japanese government, which is much interested in using the recent cultural exchange for easing the historically strained relationship between Japan and South Korea. In August 2004, the Liberal Democratic Party (LDP), the party in office, invited the director of *Winter Sonata* to a seminar on the bilateral relationship between Japan and South Korea, and the then party secretary, Shinzo Abe, who became prime minister in 2006 and again in 2012, also celebrated the development of mutual cultural exchange by referring to the popularity of the drama in his official visit to South Korea. Yet he kept his silence when the Korean president raised the question of the issue of history textbooks and the granting of voting rights for local elections to resident Koreans in Japan. In the abovementioned survey (Hayashi 2004), about a quarter of respondents said that they had become more interested in resident Koreans and their history, which is not negligible but yet much lower compared to their increasing interest in South Korea. Even worse, according to a survey conducted by *Asahi Shinbun* (August 21, 2004), regarding the question about the interests that are roused by the Korean Wave, only a few mentioned historical issues or resident Koreans.

Furthermore, it should be noted that the improvement of the image of South Korea is simultaneously occurring with the demonizing of North Korea. Since the North Korean government officially acknowledged their involvement in the abduction of Japanese nationals, there has been a massive and antagonistic media bashing of North Korea. Racist attacks have also been made against resident Koreans who identify themselves with North Korea. Female North Korea–affiliated high school students who wore Korean ethnic dress as school uniforms were assaulted in the city,[3] and a self-claimed resident North Korean boxing champion's home page had to close due to a flood of blackmail messages.

A clear divide between North and South Korea in the Japanese public perception has an influence on the recognition and naming of resident Koreans according to their belonging either to South Korea or North Korea. The naming of resident Koreans—*zainichi chousenjin* (resident North Koreans or resident Koreans in general, as *chousenjin* signifies ethnicity rather than national identification), *zainichi kankokujin* (resident South Koreans to differentiate them from resident Koreans who identify themselves with North Korea), or *zainichi kankoku-chousenjin* (resident North and South Koreans to include both kinds of political identifications)—is highly political, as it involves the issue of political identification with two Korean countries. In either case, however, remaining as Korean nationals is important for many since it signifies resistance against the disgraceful naturalization to a Japanese national, as explained earlier. Recently, resident Korean communities have tried to be more open to diversity within and to widen membership regardless of his or her nationality or national identification. The name *zainichi Korian* has come to be widely used because of its apparent political neutrality although it is also criticized for the very same reason. In addition, the term has the merit of making it possible to include those who have been naturalized to Japanese as the emphasis is put more on historically embedded "Koreanness" than on national identification or the kind of passport a person has.

However, with the advent of the Korean Wave, the reference to resident South Koreans (*zainichi kankokujin*) has become used more often than before in Japanese media. The new categorization of South Korean nationals living in Japan does not just accompany the suppression of resident Koreans who identify themselves with North Korea. No less important, this manner of naming signifies an ahistorical recognition of resident Koreans that is apt to understand their existence in association with the contemporary culture and society of the nation-state called South Korea, which now produces attractive media cultures. For example, in a book titled *I Want to Know That Person's Country, South Korea* (2004), there is a small section about resident South Koreans, which is included in the chapter on the history of South Korea. The author of this section is a resident Korean, and she introduces the ambivalent identity of resident Koreans who do not clearly belong to either nation in a positive manner. However, such an approving account of ambivalent identity construction embraced in the lives of resident Koreans is diminished by the book editor's categorization of their experiences as those of the people of South Korea. In this instance, *zainichi kankokujin* does not signify resident South Koreans as much as South Korean nationals living in Japan in an ahistorical and nationalized framework. Crucial in this nationalized recognition of resident Koreans is the disregard of the collective historical memories and experiences that are shared regardless of nationality and that have been passed down from generation to generation. In the last scene of the popular film *Go* (2001), the protagonist, a third-generation resident Korean man shouts to his Japanese lover when she calls him a resident South Korean, "You Japanese do not feel at ease unless you categorize and name us in any way. Do not confine me in such a narrow category." This line, which strongly rejects the effortless categorization of resident Koreans, takes on a more imperative meaning with the advent of the Korean Wave in Japan.

TOKYO WANKEI AND THE REPRESENTATION OF RESIDENT KOREANS IN JAPAN

While there are positive impacts of the Korean Wave on the social recognition and positioning of resident Koreans in Japan, there can be discerned a confusion in the understanding their existence through the prism of South Korea, which accompanies the segregation of shared historical experiences of resident Koreans. How the Korean Wave has constructively and unconstructively impacted media representations and recognition of resident Koreans is elucidated in the TV drama series *Tokyo Wankei* (Fuji TV, Monday, 9–10 p.m.), which was broadcast from July to September 2004. The drama is about the romantic relationship between a third-generation resident South Korean woman and a Japanese man and their aspiration to overcome the obstacle of ethnic difference. The story begins with a scene in which the depressed heroine sends a message to a website from a mobile phone, "Please find the real me." This is the key word of the drama and the motif that signifies the heroine's desire to be recognized and loved just as she is, as a woman who was born in Japan of Korean ancestry. The production of the drama was clearly motivated by the recent popularity of South Korean TV dramas and films, as the producer clearly acknowledged. The drama is epoch-making in that it is the first TV drama series in prime time of a major commercial TV station that features a resident Korean as the protagonist. This testifies to another positive impact of the Korean Wave on media representations of resident Koreans, whose existence has long tended to be disregarded in the mainstream media.

However, the drama effortlessly uses resident Koreans as spice to the story in terms of acting as a hindrance to the relationship. In the drama, the story revolves around the anguish of a third-generation daughter whose economically successful second-generation father stubbornly insists on her marrying resident Koreans and opposes her wish to marry a Japanese man. He is very concerned with the historically constituted discrimination against resident Koreans in Japan. At the same time, he has a bitter memory of his dead wife's passionate but tragic relationship with a Japanese man before their marriage and how she never forgot her sense of longing for him. To him, the daughter appears to fatefully follow her mother's forbidden love relations with Japanese men. While parents' opposition to their children's marriage with Japanese nationals might, to some extent, reflect the real-life experiences of resident Koreans, the drama depicts the issue with an exclusive focus on the personal distress of resident Koreans without giving due attention to the structured discrimination in Japanese society. Issues are reduced to the personal anguish of well-to-do Korean residents in Japan, and social and historical issues are separated from the personal. Furthermore, the stubborn closedness of the resident Korean community is to blame for the daughter's agony, as symbolized by her father, who is represented as ethnocentric and obstinate and who thus cannot understand the developing relationship between Japan and South Korea. It is as if resident Koreans were all responsible for drawing the sharp, exclusive line between Japanese and resident Koreans.

In relation to this, the protagonist's distress is depicted as the clear divide between the two nations. Japan's relationship with South Korea and its people is again confounded with that of resident Koreans, whose historically contextualized experiences and subjectivities are thus interpreted in terms of those of South Korean nationality. This is shown by the catchphrase of the drama, "The love that transcends the national boundaries between Japan and South Korea." The father of the heroine often states that there is a deep gulf between Japan and Korea that is sharply divided by the Sea of Japan. Even a South Korean star who acts in *Winter Sonata* appears in the end of one episode to send a message to the audiences that people of both nations will be best friends by going beyond what happened in the past.

This displays a striking confusion between South Koreans and resident Koreans in Japan, as one viewer sharply criticized on the website:

> I think the issue of resident Koreans needs to be distinguished from the Korean Wave in Japan. Maybe they have the same nationality. Yet how is it plausible to deal with those Koreans who have been brought up in South Korea and those third generation resident Koreans who have been brought up in Japan on par? . . . It is very good in any case that the neighboring country South Korea is in the media limelight and the friendship between Japan and South Korea is being deepened. However, resident Koreans are someone living next to you, not in the neighboring country. They might be your neighbors, colleagues or friends, if you are not aware of this. No sea divides Japan and resident Koreans.[4]

Yet, looking into the official website of the drama series, most audiences' contributions seem to affirm the drama narrative of an inter-national relationship between Japan and South Korea: "Unexpectedly, I am addicted to the drama because it deals with the contemporary issues between Japan and

South Korea that we are currently embracing"; "This drama aims to bring Japan and South Korea closer, doesn't it? If so, unless the drama has a happy ending, the relationship between the two nations will remain distant"; "I am deeply impressed with the drama, which depicts the loves who struggle to overcome national boundaries."[5] These messages suggest that many audiences expect the drama series to contribute to the further improvement of the relationship between Japan and South Korea at the expense of understanding the complexity of experiences and social positioning of resident Koreans, as they are reduced to those of South Korean nationals living in Japan.

While the desire for suppressing the fallacy of racial and cultural homogeneity in Japan appears in the form of a subjectless multiculturalism in the case of the consumption of Vietnamese culture, *Tokyo Wankei* confers a kind of social recognition to resident Koreans that renders them easily consumable historical subjects through interpolating them as South Korean nationals. The positive image of South Korea that the Korean Wave promotes eventually works to newly marginalize and suppress postcolonial complexity and predicament embodied in the historical subjectivity called "resident Koreans." This is an attempt to conveniently understand her or his precarious experience and identity formation, which resist clear categorization in any sense since they are constructed in the situation in which she or he is forced to live with the deep-seated feeling of uneasiness and strain in Japanese society. Social recognition is given only when historical nuisance is tamed by and for the majority. While showing new positive developments about the social recognition of resident Koreans in Japan, the representation of resident Koreans in the drama nevertheless displays postcolonialism without history. The past is acknowledged as something that has gone and that no longer determines the present, an acknowledgment of the past not to remember but to leave behind.

The drama thus displays the replacement of multiculturalism by a banal inter-nationalism that attempts to understand the issue of multiculturalism in terms of nationality as a unit of analysis. The existence of resident Koreans in Japan is grasped from the viewpoint of the inter-national relationship between Japan and South Korea, which disregards those whose experience and identity formation are torn between the two nations. The existence of South Korean nationals living in Japan rather than resident Koreans in Japan can be publicly recognized, as they are more tolerable foreign nationals who are safely separated from the past, present, and future of the Japanese imagined community. The factual mark of difference in terms of nationality and passport, the lack of the right to vote, and the lingering difficulty of marrying Japanese nationals are dealt with in the drama but not in a way in which the myth of Japanese homogeneity, which has severely marginalized resident Koreans, is fundamentally questioned. This is reminiscent of the Japanese government's recent encouragement for resident Koreans to acquire Japanese nationality. As Eika Tai (2004) warns, even if the naturalization process becomes softer and resident Koreans can more easily "come out" by publicly using Korean names and/or acknowledging his or her ethnic roots, this does not ensure the acceptance of resident Koreans as full citizens. Unless the lingering social discriminations and the racially and ethnically essentialist definition of "Japanese" are seriously overcome, as Tai (2004, 369) argues, "resident Koreans are encouraged to 'come out', but only in a contained way" and the naturalization with Korean ethnic marks would result in their assimilation "only as a second-class Japanese."

CRITIQUE TOWARD THE FOSTERING OF CROSS-BORDER DIALOGUE

My critical analysis of the impact of the Korean Wave on the social positioning and recognition of resident Koreans in Japan should not be taken as totally rejecting positive changes. Critique is a necessary detour to further the potentiality of the emergent change and to actualize transnational dialogue through media consumption. Thus, it is no less imperative to carefully attend to the sign of change as well. Pessimism of the intellect needs to be embraced by optimism of the will. It should not be dismissed that the Korean Wave, especially the popularity of *Winter Sonata*, has made Japanese people understand South Korea and resident Koreans in a much deeper manner than before. Let me end my arguments by looking at such promising signs in audiences' responses to *Tokyo Wankei* on the show's website.

Tokyo Wankei was discussed on the fan sites of *Winter Sonata*, too.[6] Apparently the fans were motivated to watch the drama by their interest in how its production was influenced by *Winter Sonata*, but there were also many comments on the issues of social discrimination against resident Koreans, such as the historical dis/continuity, the adaptation of Japanese names, and the categorization as "resident Koreans." One person who began the discussion was so overwhelmed by the intensity of discussion that followed that she concluded that she would like to keep on studying the history of the two countries and how it had had significant impacts on resident Koreans in Japan. While, as she states, the vivacity of the discussion itself is the impact of *Winter Sonata*, the production and consumption interaction of the two dramas—*Winter Sonata* and *Tokyo Wankei*—actually positively urge audiences to rethink the history of Japanese colonialism and resident Koreans in Japan.

On the official site of *Tokyo Wankei* organized by Fuji TV, there are also some insightful comments about the relationship between *Winter Sonata* and *Tokyo Wankei*:

> Watching the drama, I came to think more about the historical relationship between Japan and South Korea. I am a Japanese who is sick of the recent Korean boom. . . . Its craze looks so superficial, and I thought that there was no consideration regarding history. . . . It is not *Winter Sonata* but *Tokyo Wankei* that roused my interest in the history of Japan and South Korea.

> I am also a third-generation resident Korean and attending a Korean school. To tell the truth, I have some reservations about the recent Korean boom in Japan. I am frustrated with the craze of Japanese people who do not even know about our history. . . . But *Tokyo Wankei* changed my view. We should try to let such people know about us!!

The positive suggestion to the latter comment, which is apparently expressed by a young female resident Korean, to educate Japanese people about history and resident Koreans should not be regarded as a one-way appeal from resident Koreans. Such an attitude would easily lead to the evasion of responsibility by the majority, who are inclined to effortlessly ask the minority to teach them what to do. Her comment should be read as an appeal for both Japanese and resident Koreans to work together. She might have been encouraged by the fact that the Japanese mass media produced a drama that dealt with the anguish of young resident Koreans as well as by reading various comments on the website that are critical of the current situation in Japan. In any case, her expression of hope embodies the possibility of cultivating a new kind of alliance through the consumption of media culture.

Similarly, many resident Koreans who sympathetically identify themselves with the protagonists express a sense of empowerment when watching the drama:

> I am myself a third-generation resident Korean and had the same experience of the breakdown of marriage with a Japanese man. So the drama does not look like another person's affair. . . . I was also distressed about who I am but could not tell any of my Japanese friends of my anguish of living as a resident Korean in Japan. But I now feel healed by the drama.

> I am also a third-generation resident Korean. I am really empowered by the drama—having two homelands is a nice thing. . . . Thanks a lot.

> I have never felt it wonderful to be born a resident Korean, but the drama encourages me to face what I am. Thanks to all the production staff for giving me a touching story.

While these comments make us realize the significance of the drama that deals with the hitherto disregarded issue about resident Koreans, there are also comments critical of the drama, arguing that it fails to attend to the complexity of the lives and existence of resident Koreans by confounding

South Koreans and resident Koreans and that the drama lacks historical depth.

> I am ambivalent about the recent Korean boom. I am glad that many people have more interests in South Korea but they still continue to be uninformed of resident Koreans. The drama story is nice but it is still far from our reality, as it is depicted from a Japanese point of view.

> I had quite a mixed feeling when I first watched this drama. . . . My grand-father was forcibly brought to Japan during the colonial rule. There are many children and grandchildren of such people living in Japan. Young people would think that such old incidents are none of their business, but at least for the first generation resident Koreans it is not something of the past that is finished. The recent Korean Wave has improved the relationship between South Korea and Japan. To further mutual understanding, the history needs to be more firmly grasped. I am sure that the drama has let many Japanese people know about resident Koreans whose existence has long been out of the front stage of Japanese society (but, let me remind you, not as foreign nationals who are living in Japan but as resident Koreans who are living traces of a tragic history). Still now, it is not easy for resident Koreans to rent an apartment. Fact is stranger than fiction. There are more intricate troubles and incidents in reality. I wish those who watch *Tokyo Wankei* will become more interested in resident Koreans. And I wish more dramas will be produced that deal with the issue of resident Koreans.

The coexistence of divergent views on *Tokyo Wankei* expressed by resident Koreans is a testimony of the diverse social positions and experiences of resident Koreans who cannot be understood as a homogeneous ethnic group. However, either positive or negative, they are expressed by someone who has long been positioned as a second-rate citizen in Japanese society. We need to understand the complexity and the depth of the issues by seriously listening to the voices of resident Koreans who sympathetically find their anguish and hope in the drama, without effortlessly celebrating the empowering effect of the drama.

> None of my good friends knows about my ethnic roots. I always fear that they would dislike me if they knew that fact. I was really moved by the scene where Mika [the protagonist] confesses her ethnic background and nationality to her lover. I had the same experience once. I was moved to tears. . . . I really wish for a happy ending.

Needless to say, her tears do not simply testify to the positive impact of the Korean Wave or the moving narrative of the love story. It is a historical present of resident Koreans living with the lingering structure of social dis-crimination that gives a special power to the drama narrative.

Answering the wishes of many audiences, the drama has a happy ending. Yet, the previous person's wish for a happy ending is not of the same kind as that of Japanese audiences. Here lies the expectation for real life. No matter how strongly resident Koreans are empowered by the drama and the Korean Wave in Japan, the crucial question still remains as to how to substantiate the sense of empowerment by making actual social transformation. The above-mentioned appeal of "let's work together" by a resident Korean needs to be more actively made from the people whose social positions are more privileged. For this purpose, a critical examination of how the transnational media flows intersect the postcolonial and the multicultural is imperative.

NOTES

1. For a detailed analysis of the Hong Kong boom in Japan in the 1990s, see chapter 5 of Iwabuchi (2002a).

2. For details see Ryang (2000) and Tai (2004).

3. The uniforms are modeled after traditional Korean costumes and the female students' Korean origins are easily recognizable by the uniform.

4. See www.myprofile.ne.jp/blog/archive/acquire-mind/25 (site discontinued, last accessed November 30, 2007).

5. See wwwc.fujitv.co.jp/wankei/index2.html (site discontinued, last accessed November 30, 2007).

6. See www.innolife.net/bbs2/list.php?bbs=bbs1&pg=25 (site discontinued, last accessed November 30, 2007).

Chapter Six

East Asian Media Culture, Inter-Asian Referencing, and Cross-Border Dialogue

In the last two decades, we have witnessed dramatic developments in the production of media cultures and their transnational circulation in many parts of the world. East Asia is one of the key regions in which these alternative cultural expressions flourish, in which cultural mixing and corporate collaboration are intensifying, and in which intraregional consumption has been set in motion, as I have analyzed with regard to the Korean Wave in Japan in the previous chapter. Accordingly, the studies of East Asian media cultures and their intraregional circulation have been growing considerably. Innovatively examining such cultural dynamics, many works have elucidated the new kinds of cultural creativities and connections that have been advanced beyond national borders. Inter-Asian referencing is one significant approach for innovatively making sense of the rise of media and culture flows and connections. It enables us to critically reexamine approaches and theories that are derived from Euro-American experiences in East Asian contexts as it makes concepts and theories derived from Asian experiences translocally relevant and shared, as well as developing a nuanced comprehension of Asian experiences through a reciprocal cross-border learning process.

Furthermore, inter-Asian referencing is significant because it has become an integral part of the production and consumption of media culture in the region. As such, inter-Asian referencing is not just a matter of academic theorization but is now part of people's mundane practice of meeting Asian neighbors, making a reference to other Asian modernities, and cultivating cross-border dialogue. Revisiting the studies of East Asian media and cultural flows and connections, this chapter discusses the great potentials of the transgressive cross-border dialogue that they have been fostering and at the same time points out the drawback posed by market-driven media and cultural globalization.

FROM DE-WESTERNIZATION TO
INTER-ASIAN REFERENCING

While the necessity of de-Westernizing academic knowledge production in media and cultural studies has been advocated (e.g., Curran and Park 2000), it seems to be attracting renewed academic attention. This has much to do with the latest rise of non-Western countries such as China and India and the reappearance of some deep-seated issues regarding the de-Westernization of academic knowledge. For example, a conference titled "Beyond 'Center' and 'Periphery': (De-)Westernization in International and Intercultural Communication," held in 2011 at the University of Erfurt in Germany, states the purpose of the conference as follows:

> As part of the globalization discourse, emerging research areas such as India, China, Africa or Latin America, once deemed peripheral, have increasingly come into focus. However, the available methods and analytical models turned out to be insufficient for explaining media use or media effects in those regions. But does a genuinely non-Western type of media and communication research truly exist? Ironically, even the critical examination of Western models and the call for the "de-Westernization" of media studies have largely been voiced by Western researchers. And on the other hand, is the dominance of Western theories and methodological approaches primarily rooted in cultural imperialism, or have these research paradigms evolved and proven fruitful in many cases of international and intercultural communication studies? After all, the paradigms emerging from the Euro-American space have been subjected to critical analysis and improvement rather than outright rejection. (Conference of the International and Intercultural Communication 2011)

Being open and critical, the conference statement displays some important issues regarding the de-Westernization of knowledge production. First of all, it underscores a problematic that the prefix "de-" tends to indicate a rejection with "either-or" inference (Sabry 2009). It is indeed unproductive and even absurd to think that the application of theories derived from Euro-American experiences to non-Western contexts should be totally rejected. Theory has a translocal, if not universal, applicability. But being conceptualized based on experiences and realities of a particular location in a specific historical situation, theory always requires a subtle spatiotemporal translation whenever we apply it to a concrete phenomenon in a specific context. This is true even with the application of theories to the context in which those theories were originally conceptualized, much more with different sociohistorical contexts.

In this sense, it is incongruous to put any spatial and geographical adjective to theory. There are no genuine Western theories any more than there are genuine Asian theories. It cannot be denied that theories derived from some Euro-American experiences predominate the production of knowledge in the world. The boosting Anglophone hegemony in academia has further pushed this tendency. If we look at the major theoretical references in the works of media and cultural studies in Asia (including mine!), we would never fail to realize the weighty presence of academic concepts and theorization by scholars working in Euro-American contexts such as Hall, Foucault, Butler, Said, and so on. However, this does not necessarily mean the uncritical one-way application of "Western theories" into other contexts. Rather, as clearly shown by the recent development of media and cultural studies in non-Western regions, they display a creative practice of the provincialization of "Western theories" through critical translation (Chakrabarty 2000). Such a creative act of appropriation and translation of theories derived from experiences of Western societies works well to understand what is going on in non-Western regions. Moreover, such critical interrogation and innovative application is helpful to refine and further develop theories derived from Western experiences, as well as to construct innovative theories derived from non-Western contexts if they are well combined with a subtly nuanced examination of specific non-Western experiences. This kind of engagement with "Western theories" needs to be clearly differentiated from an automatic one-way application of theories derived from Euro-American experiences or a parochial claim of establishing "Asian theories" vis-à-vis "Western theories."

However, while much is made of a self-critical call to de-Westernization of knowledge production by various scholars over the world, provincialization is not easy either, as we are all implicated in a firmly structured uneven binary of "Western theory and non-Western derivative experience," hence a continuing call for de-Westernization. Especially pressing is the question of reciprocal listening. What is at issue here is how cultural studies scholars working in Euro-American contexts read works in other contexts while cultural studies scholars working in non-Euro-American contexts tend to regularly read works in Euro-American contexts as theoretical references. Raka Shome (2010, 700) points out in her critical discussion of the internationalization of cultural studies that even when "non-Western theories" capture international attention, they still tend to be considered as a revisionary moment for the original Euro-American ones, which "implicitly re-iterates the otherness of the international in relation to the US/UK axis of cultural studies." A turn to "the ex-periphery" thus often indicates the underlying perception of temporal gap in the guise of an appreciation of a critical application of theories derived from Western experiences to non-Western contexts. Daya Thussu (2009) argues that academic institutions and researchers in Western countries often deal with non-Western cases as an alibi for their internationalizing posture without truly earnest efforts to go beyond the existing West-centric hierarchy in knowledge production. In this regard, attending to what happened to the rise of "the ex-periphery" in the past would be beneficial. The rise of "India, China, Africa or Latin America" is indeed a matter of immediacy now, but has a similar call for de-Westernization been made regarding the rise of Japan, Hong Kong, or South Korea in the last twenty or thirty years? If so, what has been discussed and whether and how have we not succeeded in de-Westernizing the production of knowledge then? A serious effort of historicization would rescue the current call for the de-Westernization of knowledge production from becoming a never-ending project, which eventually verifies the continuing hegemony of the Euro-American production of knowledge.

Both scholars working in Euro-American contexts and those in other contexts are all responsible for reproducing this politics of not listening. In respect to this, an identified "irony" in the above statement that "the call for the de-Westernization of media studies has largely been voiced by Western researchers" suggests some intriguing points. It suggests that scholars working in and on non-Western contexts are responsible for a politics of not listening too, as those scholars mostly read theories and researches developed in Western countries and uncritically apply them to non-Western cases and contexts. It can also be argued, however, that the irony actually implies the disinclination of scholars critically working in and on non-Western contexts—regardless of his or her nationality or ethnicity—to engage in the existing framework of de-Westernization. They might stay out of the fallacy of claiming "pure" non-Western theory as well as a structured predicament of engaging an imperative issue of how to learn from other experiences in a reciprocal and dialogic manner. At the same time, we should not ignore the fact that there were actually many calls for de-Westernization by scholars working in non-Western regions in the last decade.[1] And there have been some deliberate attempts and practices in the field of media and cultural studies by researchers working in and on Asia without referring to the term *de-Westernization*. Here, a key term is *inter-Asian referencing*.

Inter-Asian referencing aims to advance the innovative production of knowledge through reciprocal learning from other Asian experiences. It is a self-critical strategic call to activate dialogue among hitherto internationally unattended scholarly works of Asian regions—though still mostly limited to English-language works, which is an imperative issue beyond the scope of this article—to go beyond a globally structured collusive disinclination to seriously attend to non-Western research. But it is not a closed-minded regionalism. In reworking the notion of "Asia as method," which was advocated by a Japanese thinker, Takeuchi Yoshimi, in the early 1960s,[2] Kuan Hsing Chen (2010, xv) offers a succinct recapitulation of his idea: "Using Asia as an imaginary anchoring point can allow societies in Asia to become one another's reference points, so that the understanding of the self can be transformed, and subjectivity rebuilt." This will lead to the construction of "an alternative horizon, perspective, or method for posing a different set of questions about world history" (Chen 2010, xv). Hitherto underexplored intraregional or inter-Asian comparison is considered highly meaningful for understanding modern trajectories of Asian countries in a new critical light, as it is based on shared experiences of "forced" modernization and less hierarchical relationships than the prevailing West-Asia comparison, which is based on assumed temporal distance between them.

Given that creative translation of theories derived from Western experiences in non-Western context still tends to be confined to a West-Rest paradigm, inter-Asian referencing strategically aims to go beyond this predicament by promoting dialogue among diverse voices and perspectives derived and developed in Asian contexts. However, this is not to elucidate modern Asian experiences in an essentialist term in contrast to and/or separate from Western and other non-Western experiences. By "reembracing" deep-seated Western inflections on Asian experiences, an inspired inter-Asian comparison and referencing aims to refreshingly elucidate and theorize specific processes in which the experiences of Asian modernizations have been formulated, whereby the production of knowledge derived from Asian experiences leads to the articulation of visions and values translocally relevant for transmuting not just Asian societies but also European societies and the world as a whole. As such, the idea of Asia as method and inter-Asian referencing must be distinguished from parochial regionalism as it does not exclude researchers working in and on contexts outside of Asia nor underestimate the significance of transnational collaboration between them either. It can be considered a productive detour to provincialization.

"EAST ASIAN POP CULTURE STUDIES" AND INTER-ASIAN REFERENCING

Chen's suggestion reflects and is motivated by an innovative project of inter-Asian cultural studies in which he, along with other colleagues, has played a central role. As another key figure, Beng Huat Chua (2010), points out, one of the successfully developed fields in the project is "East Asian pop culture studies." Since the middle of 1990s, the production capacity of media cultures such as TV dramas, films, and popular music has developed considerably in East Asia. Furthermore, inter-Asian promotion and coproduction of media cultures have become commonplace through the collaboration and partnerships among media and cultural industries. These developments are suggestive of a trend that media globalization enhances regionalization.

Whether it engenders an East Asian identity is highly questionable, but we could safely say that there has emerged a loose cultural geography, as most of East Asian media cultures, with the exception of some cultures such as Japanese animation, are capitalized, circulating, and consumed predominantly, if not exclusively, in East Asia (including those migrants and diasporas living outside the region). Examining sociohistorically contextualized experiences that intersect East Asia as region, many researches have been seriously examining the cultural dynamics of production, circulation, and consumption that have been engendered under globalization processes. [3]

Reflecting on this development, Chua (2010; 2011) proposes that cultural studies scholars working in Asia should make conscious efforts to advance inter-Asian referencing in more organized manners on two levels. He contends that the development of localized (re)conceptualization and theorization in Asian contexts with refined uses of local terminologies and concepts beyond straightforward application of English concepts is required in the first place. Inter-Asian referencing renders such concepts not just unique to one particular (non-Western) location but translocally applicable and disseminated. One example he refers to is Sun Jung's (2011) conceptualization of *"mugukjeok"* in the South Korean context, which he thinks offers a more nuanced meaning of "positive quality of mobility, of being unbounded by nations" than an English term such as *transnational* (Chua 2011, 44). Jung develops the concept by referring to the notion of *mukokuseki*, which I conceptualized in the Japanese context. As I discussed elsewhere (Iwabuchi 2002a, 28), *"mukokuseki* literally means something or someone lacking any nationality, but also implies the erasure of racial or ethnic characteristics or a context, which does not imprint a particular culture or country with these features." Such erasure is intentionally or unintentionally made in the processes of cultural mixing and juxtaposition of multiple "local" and "foreign" elements (the term *mukokuseki* was first coined in the early 1960s to describe a new action-film genre in Japan that parodied Hollywood Western films such as *Shane*). I used the Japanese concept to discuss how some Japanese animations and video games that did not really represent tangible ethnocultural characteristics of Japan had become well received in many parts of the world. Referring to my conceptualization of *mukokuseki*, Jung (2011) further develops the notion in her analysis of the rise of South Korean media culture, using an equivalent Korean term, *mugukjeok*. Jung explicates the process of cultural mixing and transculturation of "Koreanness" (especially in terms of masculinity) in South Korea and discusses how it enhances the cross-border mobility of South Korean media culture, including pop stars and films. Jung's inter-Asian referencing expands the notion of *mukokuseki* in two interrelated senses: First of all, it makes the conceptualization translocally relevant and applicable to wider ranges of media culture. More significantly, it also shows how attending to a similar and different experience in East

Asia generates a sophisticated understanding of the interaction between transculturation and cross-border mobility of media cultures, which is in turn applied and further developed outside South Korea (not limited to Asian regions). It is this mutual learning process that makes inter-Asian referencing contribute to the innovative production of knowledge.

In order to make such inter-Asian referencing more active and systematic in the study of East Asian media and cultural connections, it is necessary to historicize whether and how media culture production, circulation, and consumption have been materializing a cultural geography of East Asia. Younghan Cho (2011), who also proposes the advancement of East Asian pop culture studies, argues that the historicization of East Asian pop culture in terms of colonial connections as well as the influence of Hong Kong and Japanese media culture on other parts of East Asia in the last thirty or forty years is crucial to fully comprehend the commonality and specificity of the current popularity of South Korean media cultures. Spatiotemporal comparison with other East Asian media cultures and the examination of inter-Asian influences would urge us to consider the Korean Wave, among other East Asian counterparts, "as the iteration of East Asian pop culture" (Cho 2011, 388). Cho argues that the idea of iteration, which is repetition with a difference, is important to deessentialize and radically pluralize the conception of "region." This idea is clearly expressed by Gayatri Spivak (2008), that "different histories, languages, and idioms 'that come forth' each time we try to add an 's' to the wish for a unified originary name" (quoted in Duara 2010). The idea of iteration urges us to make sense of the rise of South Korean media culture not as a uniquely unique South Korean phenomenon but in terms of "the historicity as well as the multiplicity of East Asian pop culture" (Cho 2011, 388).

One issue that the historicization of East Asian media culture would productively elucidate is cultural mixing and adaptation in terms of two associated processes: East Asian media culture's negotiation with American counterparts and the interchange between East Asian media cultures. East Asian media cultures have long dexterously hybridized in local elements while absorbing American cultural influences. The analysis of this process is crucial in order to evade both an essentialist view of Asian values and traditions and a simplified view of American cultural domination. It shows at once the operation of global power configurations in which Euro-American culture has played a central role and the active cultural translation practices in the non-West. Many studies have discussed how East Asian countries have subtly hybridized American media cultures in terms of production techniques, representational genres, and comparative consumption (e.g., Lee 1991; Iwabuchi 2002a; Shim 2006), but a comprehensive examination of similar and different experiences of negotiation with American media culture in, for example, Hong Kong, Japan, and South Korea has not yet been substantially conducted. Instead, we still find the repeated statement that Asian media culture "translate Western or American culture to fit Asian tastes" (Ryoo 2009, 145). Such comparative analysis would explicate the continuum of cultural mixing and adaptation in East Asia, ranging from creative translation that produces something new, selective appropriation of Western cultures, subtle reformulation of local cultures, eventual replication based on global mass culture formats, reessentialization of cultural difference between the West and Asia, and the nationalist discourse of the excellence of cultural indigenization (Iwabuchi 2002a; Cho 2011).

Cultural mixing and adaptation has also been occurring among East Asian media cultures, especially in terms of the influences of Hong Kong, Japanese, and, more recently, South Korean media cultures. And this also has become a conspicuous constituent of the production of media culture in East Asia as East Asian media culture markets have become synchronized, and producers, directors, actors, as well as capital from around the region, have been working across national borders.[4] Remakes of successful TV dramas and films from other parts of East Asia are frequently produced, especially between Japanese, South Korean, Hong Kong, and Taiwanese media texts, and Japanese comic series are often adapted for TV dramas and films outside of Japan. The analysis of the dynamic processes of intertextual reworking as well as inter-Asian cultural adaptation intriguingly exposes both commonality and difference in the constitution and representation of "East Asian modernity."

A prominent example is *Meteor Garden* (*Liuxing Huayuan*), a Taiwanese TV drama series that adopts a Japanese comic series. The drama series became very popular in many parts of East and Southeast Asia, so much so that Japanese and South Korean versions were later produced. Most recently an unofficial Chinese version was also created. A chain of adaptations of the same story of girls' comic series (*shojo manga*), *Hana yori dango*, which has been widely read in East Asia, shows some kind of regional sharedness. It is a story about confrontation, friendship, and love between an ordinary female high school student and four extraordinary, rich, and good-looking male students. While the representation of beautiful boys in each version is a very important factor for its popularity (Jung 2010), the common motif also travels well across East Asia and Southeast Asia, which is a *shojo* narrative. As Lan Xuan Le (2009, 35) argues, the *shojo* narrative mostly "revolves around the border crisis when *shojo* heroines symbolically cross out of girlhood—the heroine's first love." It is "an ambivalent and resistant genre that narratively and stylistically defers incipient womanhood—and its attendant responsibilities—by maintaining the open-ended possibility of adolescence" (2009, 82). However, inter-Asian adaptation of the *shojo* narrative also engenders divergence. Among other narratives such as family relationship, Confucian values, and masculinity an intriguing difference is discerned in the representation of the agency of the adolescent heroine. As the fanciful and nostalgic representation of female agency in the negotiation with adolescent transition is a key to the genre, "the *shojo* heroine is always, in one way or another, active, agentive, and engaged against both the villains of her narrative and the social ills that created them" (Le 2009, 35). However, in the South Korean version of *Boys over Flowers*, the agency of the young female being is, as Le argues, overwhelmed by the "'spectacles of suffering' which marks the heroine's 'enunciative passivity'" (43). This divergence from the original story and the other two versions of the drama series can be explained by the predominance of melodramatic narrative in South Korea, which has been historically constituted through its traumatic experiences of Japanese colonialism, postwar turmoil, and brutally compressed modernization. Nevertheless, despite the difference and inflection that are articulated in the country's specific sociohistorical context, each drama "remains definitely Asian in its inflection" as all versions still share "the imagery of Asian modern" that is narrated through the experience of female adolescence (Le 2009, 115). Inter-Asian adaptation work as a channel though which the intricate juxtaposition of specificity and commonality of East Asian modernities is freshly articulated.

INTER-ASIAN REFERENCING AS MUNDANE PRACTICE

Even more significantly, inter-Asian referencing has also become an integral part of people's mundane experiences of consuming media cultures. In East Asia, the consumption of media cultures such as TV dramas and films from other parts of the region has become more commonplace in the last twenty years. For the most part, this development was something that the producers were not conscious of and did not expect in the production process, since media cultures are produced chiefly for national audiences. However, media cultures have transcended national boundaries to reach unforeseen audiences via free-to-air channels, cable and satellite channels, pirated VHS tapes and DVDs, and Internet streaming. Furthermore, increasing numbers of media cultures have come to be produced and coproduced to target those international audiences. While Internet sites and various social media are undoubtedly the most immediate vehicles for transnational mediated communications, the inter-Asian circulation of media cultures such as TV programs, films, popular music, and comics has significantly facilitated cross-border exchange. Many studies have examined how inter-Asian media culture consumption has brought about new kinds of cross-border relationships and people's perception of self and other (Asians) and their similarities and differences self-reflexively, sympathetically, and/or orientalizingly on a large scale that has never been observed before (e.g., Chua and Iwabuchi 2008; Iwabuchi 2002a, 2004a; Kim 2008).

Against this background, Cho (2011) further proposes to develop a systematic collation and theorization of various patterns of people's experiences of mediated inter-Asian referencing. For Cho (2011, 393), this is to theorize "East Asian sensibilities" in order to clarify emerging "identities, consciousnesses, and mentalities within its cultural geography" in a way akin to Williams's idea of "structure of feeling." While the term *sensibilities* runs the risk of signifying an unnecessarily exclusive boundedness of East Asian experiences, East Asian sensibilities should not be considered static or evenly shared but marked by "its asymmetric but synchronous spatialities and its uneven but simultaneous temporalities" (Cho 2011, 394). The mixed perception of spatiotemporal sameness and difference, closeness and distance, and familiarity and strangeness constitutes such sensibilities.

As a corollary of the advancement of cultural globalization, as Ien Ang and Jon Stratton (1996, 22–24) argue, we have come to live in "a world where all cultures are both (like) 'us' and (not like) 'us,'" one where "familiar difference" and "bizarre sameness" are simultaneously articulated in multiple ways through the unpredictable dynamic of uneven global cultural encounters and are engendering a complex perception of cultural distance. East Asian media and cultural connections have promoted such a sense of cultural resonance among people in the region who meet cultural neighbors vis-à-vis a common but different experience of constructing a vernacular modernity. Similar and dissimilar, different and same, close and distant, fantasizing and realistic, all of these intertwined perceptions subtly intersect so as to arouse a sense of cultural identification, relatedness, and sharedness in the eyes of East Asian people. The mediated encounter with other Asian modernities makes many people in East Asia mutually appreciate how the common experiences of modernization, urbanization, Westernization, and globalization are similarly and differently experienced in other East Asian contexts and realize that they now inhabit the same developmental time zone with other parts of East Asia.

As media cultures of various places regularly cross national boundaries, people now have a much wider repertoire for reflecting on their own lives and sociopolitical issues, while the national mass media are still the most powerful in this respect. Sympathetic watching of Japanese or South Korean TV dramas has, for example, encouraged audiences in various East Asian countries to have a fresh view of gender relations, lives of the youth, and justice in their own societies through the perception of the spatial-temporal distance and closeness of other East Asian modernities (Chua and Iwabuchi 2008). As discussed in chapter 5, even though the sense of nostalgia, which is often evoked by the consumption of media culture from other Asian countries, might reproduce Orientalist views of other Asians as "not quite as modern as us" by equating "their" present with "our" past, nostalgia also might work to evoke self-reflexive thinking. Inter-Asian media and cultural connections thus work as a great opportunity for many people to critically review the state of their own culture, society, and historical relationship with other parts of Asia. Media culture plays a significant role in constructing the national public. Many studies have shown how the mass media, such as film, radio, and TV, have constructed imagined communities and the public sphere on a national level. However, as media cultures of various places regularly cross national boundaries, transnational media flows are also playing an important role in this process. Inter-Asian media culture circulation has come to gain weight as it has given a wide range of resources for people's public engagement in everyday life. People's participation in the public realm via the media is not just limited to a Habermasian public sphere, but mundane meaning construction through media consumption is an indispensable part of it (Livingstone 2005). Emotion and affection are also vital to people's participation in and belonging to society, and the consumption of media cultures plays a significant part in constituting the cultural public sphere, which "provides vehicles for thought and feeling, for imagination and disputatious argument, which are not necessarily of inherent merit but may be of some consequence" (McGuigan 2005, 435). It would be too premature to see the emergence of cultural public spheres in East Asia, but inter-Asian referencing via East Asian media cultures has newly brought about cross-border dialogue: dialogue, not in the sense of actually meeting in person to talk to each other but in the sense that it encourages people to critically and self-reflexively reconsider one's own life, society, and culture, as well as sociohistorically constituted relations with and perceptions of others.

This emerging landscape of people's mundane experiences of inter-Asian referencing is reminiscent of Takeuchi's sense of pleasurable surprise that he perceived when he first visited China, a sense that triggered the formulation of the idea of Asia as method. Unlike when he visited Euro-American countries, he was then very much impressed by his observation that people's thinking, feeling, and experiences in China looked very familiar (and different) to those in Japan, as both shared a catch-up positioning and mentality of developmental temporality vis-à-vis Western counterparts. A similar sense of pleasant surprise has also pushed the development of academic research on media cultures in East Asia in the last twenty years. However, this time, that sensibility was not just derived from researchers' self-critical observation of other Asian societies. Rather, researchers, including myself, have witnessed how media and cultural connections prompt many people in the region to perceive something similar and different in the composition of modernities of other Asian societies. The development of East Asian media and cultural connections thus does not just display the possibility of inter-Asian referencing merely as a method to produce alternative academic knowledge but as a historic opportunity of engendering people's cross-border dialogue as mundane practice, which inspired researchers to avidly document, interpret, and problematize.

LIMITS AND DETERMENTS OF CROSS-BORDER DIALOGUE

If we take seriously the significance of inter-Asian referencing as a matter of the mundane promotion of mediated cross-border dialogue we need to examine both its potential and limitation of transcending the exclusionary force of controlling national-cultural borders. The previous chapter discussed a limitation of inter-Asian referencing to enhance engagement with multicultural questions, but it is required for us to more systematically examine insensibilities, disconnections, divides, and antagonisms that have been generated by East Asian media culture connectivity.

A devastating emerging trend is the exacerbation of a vicious circle of inter-Asian nationalism. The rise of soft power competition has given rise to and added fuel to the flames of antagonistic nationalism in East Asia. The regional circulation of Japanese media culture encounters the negative legacy of Japanese colonialism in terms of territorial disputes and historical memories, and that of its South Korean counterpart confronts the clash over the ownership of ancient historical narratives and traditional culture, as well as adverse responses against the cultural invasion by the Korean Wave among some populace of East Asia (see Chua 2012, 131–34). International politics such as territorial disputes and historical issues are casting a grave shadow in Japan over the East Asian circulation of media cultures and cross-border dialogue that has been developed by it. Large demonstrations against Fuji TV for broadcasting many South Korean TV dramas were organized beginning in August 2011, and the Japanese mass media subsequently refrained from broadcasting South Korean TV dramas or featuring South Korean pop singers in the programs. Instead, as public opinion surveys show the sharp ascent of anti-China and anti-Korea sentiments among the populace in 2012, various kinds of anti-Korea and anti-China books and journal articles have been published and put on the main shelves of bookshops in Japan. In relation to these developments, it needs to be noted that anti-Korean nationalism targets resident Koreans in Japan. This is shown by the popularity of a comic book titled *Anti-Korean Wave* (*Kenkanryu*). Against the trend of the Korean Wave fervor in Japan, it negatively illustrates the "truth" of South Korea, especially in terms of the "fallacy" of nationalistic posture against the history of Japanese colonialism. However, it eventually depicts resident Koreans who were born and have been brought up in Japan as representative of irrational, ignorant Koreans whose "distorted" claim of the history of Japanese colonialism is brilliantly debunked by cool, knowledgeable young Japanese people (see Liscutin 2009). The unambiguous identification of migrants and diaspora with their "home" country has engendered racist attacks against them.

The development of inter-Asian cultural public spheres also raises a question of the politics of inclusion and exclusion. While we cannot neatly generalize the division between people in terms of place of residence, class, gender, and ethnicity, inter-Asian media circulation has brought about cross-border disparity and marginalization in various overlapping ways. The disparity in the material accessibility to media culture has not gone away in Asian regions. Although the development of the Internet and cheap DVDs has encouraged a wider public consumption of various media culture from many parts of the world, a tremendous number of places and people do not yet enjoy this access to the media culture circulation due to economic restraints.

Furthermore, while research on inter-Asian media consumption has tended to be fascinated with the new ways in which media culture engenders self-reflexive dialogues, it is necessary to give more attention to the issue of marginalization and nonsharing that is accompanied and even engendered by the promotion of inter-Asian mediated referencing in a particular manner. In previous chapters, I argue the ways in which the market-driven forces of the inter-nationalized promotion of cultural exchange and diversity have been generated in ways to discourage the engagement with multicultural questions within the borders and cross-border dialogue in the Japanese context. This is also the case with the development of East Asian media and cultural connections. As discussed in chapter 5, the inter-nationalized promotion of media and cultural connection simultaneously has generated the empowerment of resident Koreans in Japan and disengagement with postcolonial and multicultural questions via the Korean Wave. An even more crucial question is what kind of media culture is encouraged to circulate and be mutually consumed. The rise of East Asian media cultures has been formulated under and incorporated into imbalanced globalization processes, in which globally configured power relations surpass a West-Asia binary and pervade both. Being promoted by a transnational alliance of media industries, most of which are based in a small number of industrialized countries, the activation of inter-Asian media culture circulation has engendered a new international hierarchy with the rise of subcenters such as Tokyo, Seoul, Hong Kong, Taipei, Singapore, Bangkok, and Shanghai. As the advancement of market-oriented industrial partnerships has facilitated a formation of inter-Asian media culture networks, the kinds of media texts that are promoted to circulate are chiefly commercially and ideologically hegemonic ones in each country, which tend not to represent socioculturally marginalized people and voices within the nation or represent them in stereotypical ways, if at all. This predisposition is also pushed by states' promotion of soft power and nation branding. Their interplay works to deter and limit cross-border dialogic connections in East Asia through the mutual highlighting of national-cultural borders while deterring the questions of cultural diversity that are not justly recognized within the nation from becoming a significant part of cross-border dialogue. Although the digital communication technologies have diversified grassroots cultural expressions and mediated cross-border connections, including those among marginalized people and activists working for them, we still need to ask what kinds of mutual understanding are predominantly promoted through which media texts, and whose voices and which issues are not included in the inter-Asian cultural public sphere.

This point is suggestive of the lacuna in the studies of inter-Asian media and cultural connections, which tend not to attend critically to the politics of representation. For example, when I conducted audience research on the South Korean TV drama series *Winter Sonata* in Japan, or the Japanese TV drama series *Tokyo Love Story* in Taiwan, more attention was paid to how audiences positively interpret the gender relations and love romances that are represented in the TV dramas from other Asian societies to self-critically reflect on their own lives and societies (see Iwabuchi 2002a; 2004a). This is still a relevant research question in studies of inter-Asian media culture consumption, but what is missing in this investigation is the critical analysis of the drama representations and the cross-examination of what kinds of representation of gender relations, for example, are traversing the boundaries in East Asia, and what kinds are not. The issues of representation are covered up by researchers' attention to audiences' self-reflexive consumption. While critical studies of queer cultures, ethnic minorities, and migrants in media representation have been much conducted in the national context, these are not yet well explored in studies of inter-Asian media and cultural connections. More rigorous analyses will need to be done in order to examine whether and how transnationally consumed texts in East Asia do justice to the cultural differences, inequality, and marginalization of each nation in terms of gender, sexuality, race, ethnicity, region, class, and migration/diasporas—whether and how cross-border media culture flows are (un)related to cross-border transgression and how cross-border dialogue can be fostered to go beyond the resilient national-cultural borders.

The above consideration raises a question about the analytical unit of inter-Asian referencing. Cho (2011) argues that cautious use of the term *national culture* would be necessary in the theorization of "East Asian pop culture." I agree that the idea of the nation is not necessarily "suppressive or even fascist enforcement that erases the diversity and multiplicity of different locales" (2011, 390). The nation-state is still a significant unit of analysis as it exerts a considerable institutional and affective power in the articulation of East Asian media and cultural connections. However, a potential risk of even a cautious deployment of "methodological nationalism" should be taken seriously as well. We need to be watchful of whether a nation-centered analysis of iteration and East Asian sensibilities might lose sight of the ways in which the highlighting of "national-territorial" similarities, differences, and interactions works to dampen our attention to sociocultural marginalization within and across the nation.

TAKING INTER-ASIAN REFERENCING SERIOUSLY

The rise of East Asian media cultures and regional connections has indisputably become a significant field of academic analysis, which merits further development since it contributes to enriching our comprehension of cultural globalization. The issues that inter-Asian referencing highlights are not limited to the transcendence of Euro-American dominance and parochial regionalism/nativism in the production of knowledge. As cross-border mediated connections have become a mundane practice in East Asia, inter-Asian referencing, in its full sense, calls for researchers working inside and outside of Asia to take seriously the progress of people's cross-border dialogue, which media and cultural connections have been cultivating.

However as the phenomenon is no longer emergent but has been more and more incorporated into the dominant structure of global power configuration, we need to rethink why "East Asia pop culture" matters and for what purpose and for whom "inter-Asian referencing" can be a useful method. Theorization of East Asian media and cultural connections would not be satisfactory if it does not pay critical attention to whether and how they interrelatedly challenge or generate inequality and marginalization within a region and nation and discourage cross-border dialogue. A nation-based inter-Asian comparison is useful to make these inquiries as long as we fundamentally problematize the supposition of national culture as a unit of cultural connection and diversity. The discussion of de-Westernization tends to overlook intraregional and intranational disconnection and disparity (Shome 2009), and this could also be the case with inter-Asian referencing in studies of East Asian media culture, which is never free from the inter-national administration of cultural diversity.

NOTES

1. As for the recent works of the de-Westernization of media and cultural studies, see, for example, Erni and Chua (2005), Thussu (2009), and Wang (2011).

2. For an English translation, see Takeuchi (2005).

3. For example, in the English-language academy, on regional cultural flows and connections: Berry, Mackintosh, and Liscutin (2009) and Kim (2008). On the Korean Wave phenomena: Chua and Iwabuchi (2008) and Cho (2005). On the popularity of Japanese media cultures: Iwabuchi (2002a, 2004a). On the rise of Chinese media cultures and markets: Fung (2008) and Curtin (2007). On fans' creative activities translating, commenting on, and conversing about

media texts that have engendered an unofficial globalization from below: Hu (2004, 2005) and Pang (2006, 2009).

4. Regarding media coproduction in East Asia, see Jin and Lee (2007) and Moran and Keane (2004).

Conclusion

This book discussed, in both the Japanese and a wider East Asian context, how the resilient force of exclusionary, delimiting national borders has gained momentum in the process of intensifying cross-border media culture flows and connections and examined several ways in which inter-national-ized modes of cultural diversity have been much encouraged while containing cultural diversity within the borders. This dual management of cultural diversity is not specific to Japan. The co-occurrence and interaction of the tightening of control of the inflow of people and multicultural situations within and the drive of promoting the outflow of media culture has been a widely observed trend in many developed countries.

On the one hand, there is a strong predisposition to control the inflows of people and manage multicultural situations out of concern for national safe-keeping and integration. Especially after the events of September 11, 2001, the security of national borders has been greatly tightened and an assimila-tionist national integration discourse has become more prevalent (e.g., Turner 2003; Fortier 2008). Multiculturalism has been explicitly blamed for en-gendering national divisiveness together with a rising sense of longing for a "good old" safe and caring community, which is provoked by a widespread anxiety with the exacerbation of unemployment, crime, and terrorism, which globalization processes are supposed to induce. On the other hand, cultural outflows are eagerly promoted by media and cultural industries and states' policies. Many countries are keen to further the international dissemination of national media cultures. Increasing international rivalry encourages states to develop cultural policies that enhance the nation's brand images and pro-mote soft power, creative industries, and cultural/public diplomacy. Media and cultural industries chiefly organize the production of media culture and its international distribution, and the expansion of the market-driven globalization of media culture has pressured the state to join them for the sake of national interest.

The intersection of the cross-border flows of people and those of media culture has been studied mostly in terms of migrants' and diasporas' media uses in the host countries and the construction of the sense of belonging to multiple societies or transnationalism. This book has shown the significance of considering how the two seemingly unconnected or disjunctive flows are eventually conjunctively managed to at once redemarcate and reinforce national-cultural borders and discourage public engagement with multicultural questions and the advancement of cross-border dialogue. This approach also underlines the unevenness of the global cultural economy. For the opposite movements, such as the requisiteness of emigration of labor forces for increasing national income and the cross-border influx of media cultures, are evidently observed in many less developed countries.

Given that the dual management of national-cultural borders has shown no sign of letting up in Japan, we need to continue to make a critical examination on how cultural diversity is recognized, approved of, and promoted in a particular manner whereby an imperative issue of making the nation-state and the world more inclusive, open, and egalitarian is seriously undermined and to discuss how to effectively tackle the current situation. It needs to be made clear that the issue at stake is not the annihilation or discounting of national borders, which is implied by the notion of postnationalism. Such an expectation is unrealistic and unproductive since the nation-state does still matter to foster sociocultural inclusiveness and democratization. As Craig Calhoun (2007) rightly argues against the detached notion of cosmopolitanism, the nation-state functions as the most important unit of collective organization and plays an indispensable role in facilitating social solidarity through which citizens resist the uneven globalization processes. Nevertheless, a fundamental question still remains: how we can make the nation-state more inclusive, dialogic, and attentive to hitherto marginalized voices without renouncing the national framework? What is required to grapple with this difficult task is the advancement of "denationalized" imagination and praxis, which, as Saskia Sassen (2005) discusses, turns our focus to the reformation of the national without negating, or taking more seriously, the significant role that the nation-state can play in serving the public interest to tackle transnationally structured problems and appreciate growing cultural diversity within national borders, and to effectively engage with the issues which the existing national framework cannot handle well. There is no simple answer to how to achieve this rather challenging project of going beyond the national without rejecting it. Reflecting on the key issues discussed in the previous chapters, in the following I attempt to make some preliminary suggestions to move forward beyond the current predicament from a broader perspective of the critical studies of media and cultural globalization and conclude by making a proposal to advance a trans-Asian collaborative project.

In the age of nation branding, to appropriate Theodor Adorno's words in his well-known writing on culture and administration (1991, 107), "whoever speaks of administration speaks of culture, whether it is in his/her interest or not." The promotion of nation branding by the industry-state alliance has widely propagated a dominant discourse on the pragmatic uses of media culture for national interests. This discursive formation conceals rather than reveals imperative issues to be dealt with in the globalized world. Given that cultural policy is moving away from social democratization, we need to bring back into cultural policy discussion the vital question of "what sense of the public interest informs contemporary cultural policy studies and creative industries discourse" (Miller 2009, 187), beyond a shallow scope of serving national interests. Regarding the promotion of media culture, this is to take seriously its full potential for making marginalized voices expressed, heard, and shared in society as well as facilitating cross-border dialogue over trans-nationally shared issues. As discussed in chapter 2, the advancement of "domestic cultural diplomacy" for the sake of the public good is one such endeavor.

Heading toward implementation, the scholars of cultural globalization, including those who are not directly engaged with cultural policy studies, should ambitiously strive even more than before for the institutionalization of alternative visions and practices in society that encourage people's mutual engagement with various aggravated issues of our time beyond the confinement of exclusive national borders and sociocultural divides. Two kinds of deacademicization will be required for this venture. First, researchers need to work hard to persuade people inside and outside of the classroom in intelligible words that ethno-cultural diversity is not a threat to national cohesion but needs to be positively embraced and a self-reflexive rethinking of the self-other relationship will enrich everyone's life and make society more caring to all members, including her- or himself. While these issues have been much discussed academically and engaged theoretically, they have not yet had much relevance to people's everyday feelings and experiences. The question of how to translate critical insights into grassroots knowledge and actual practices in everyday life remains unengaged. This poses a challenge of how to reconcile "critical" and "practical" (Ang 2005). The task of researchers would be to address awkward normative questions while creatively and intelligibly demonstrating that the usefulness of critical research is "stretched beyond the level of immediacy": "thinking more complexly and reflexively about issues is actually practical, if not here and now, then in the longer term" (Ang 2005, 482). Researchers thus need to convince the public that nothing is more practical than being critical for a long-lasting pursuit of a more inclusive and democratic society.

Researchers should also closely look at the already existing critical thoughts and practices at the grass roots and put them in the foreground in society. While mainly discussing the prevalence of the container model of the nation, the previous chapters also suggest that the intensification of cross-border cultural flows and connections mundanely engender innovative connections, imaginations, and collaborations that displace and transcend such thinking. Yet they are subtly disregarded and put in the background. Like Ulrich Beck's assertion of "banal cosmopolitanism" as mentioned in chapter 1, much effort would be required to illustrate their relevance to people's lives and firmly anchor them in society. Researchers should work hard for this to happen by re-presenting them in a charming and accessible way. It should be imaginative to present a hopeful design for an inclusive society, creative to capture the attention of a critical mass, and forbearing to cope with the existing elastic structure. These are rather difficult tasks but are indispensable for the eventual reformulation of the present state of things.

In relation to this, de-academicization is also needed in terms of researchers' commitment to playing an active role in coordinating and facilitating public dialogues. Adorno (1991, 113) expressed his hope at the end of an aforementioned essay: "Whoever makes critically and unflinchingly conscious uses of the means of administration and its institutions is still in a position to realize something which would be different from merely administrated culture." Researchers as educators are most responsible for producing such administrators, who not only work as policy experts but also live as critically minded citizens. In addition, researchers themselves need to take up the role of critical administrators who devote themselves to activating and coordinating the discussion among diverse people.

In the world of global interconnection and enormous uncertainty, so many issues and diverse voices are "sharable but not necessarily or inevitably shared" (Silverstone 2006, 91). This is arguably a complication inherent in the process of cultural globalization, and we need to keep on revisiting the politics of mediated sharedness and nonsharedness. At the same time, how various issues can be shared and conversed on among various people across divides attracts scholarly attention. One notable case is the recent discussion of cultural citizenship as a dialogic learning process. While the discussion of citizenship has focused on the formal aspects of political, civil, and social rights and the duties of the citizen, cultural citizenship first and foremost aims to seriously tackle an exclusive assumption of the membership of the nation by interrogating "who is silenced, marginalized, stereotyped and rendered invisible" and to "foster dialogue, complexity and communication in place of silence and homogeneity" (Stevenson 2003, 345). To achieve this objective, Gerard Delanty (2007) further proposes to comprehend cultural citizenship as a "learning process" to transcend and unlearn officially sanctioned dominant cultural codes, categories, and values and facilitate people's self-reflexive reformation toward the construction of a more egalitarian and inclusive society. As Delanty argues, "One of the most important dimensions of citizenship concerns the language, cultural models, narratives, discourses that people use to make sense of their society, interpret their place in it, and construct courses of action" (2007, 6). Such a learning process is not just an individual practice but a collective social praxis, for it functions as "a medium of social construction by which individual learning becomes translated and coordinated into collective learning and ultimately becomes realized in social institutions" (Delanty 2002, 66).

As translators and coordinators of critical knowledge, researchers can serve an important function in the instituting of a dialogic learning process in society in which diverse citizens personally and collectively transform themselves and foster alternative views of the self-other, the nation, and the world. In the discussion of the representation of intellectuals, Edward Said (1994) argues for an image of the "amateur" who is motivated by and committed to worldly issues in the society and sincerely contests the oppressive authority. Yet the public role of researchers is not confined to critically offering an interpretation and analysis of the complexity of what is happening in the world in an intangible manner. Researchers are also required to pursue the active role of creating public spaces and opportunities in order to enable dialogue and mutual learning among citizens across various divides, which include governments, the mass media, NGOs/NPOs, citizen activists, and individuals concerned, in order to advance the collective rethinking of the constitution of the nation and the world.

I would like to conclude by proposing a collaborative project of "trans-Asia as method" to pursue the above interventions. Cross-border circulation and intersection of various flows of capital, media culture, and people interconnect East Asia both spatially and temporally, as well as materially and imaginatively, in ways that highlight historically constituted relationships and transnationally shared emergent issues. As discussed in chapters 5 and 6, the development of East Asian media and cultural connections shows great capabilities of self-reflexive inter-Asian referencing to diverse East Asian experiences for advancing people's cross-border dialogue and mutual learning as mundane practice across various divides toward the construction of an inclusive society of various levels—locally, nationally, regionally, and globally.

"Trans-Asia as method" aims to further advance such radical potentials. Let us be reminded of Kuan Hsing Chen's point that "'Asia as method' ceases to look at Asia as object of analysis" (Chen 2005, 141). The method in "Asia as method" suggests less a pure academic methodology than a means by which to engender alternative modes of knowledge production that enable us to tackle and transform the existing unequal composition of the world. Which is to say, what is required is to conjointly advance two kinds of inter-

Asian referencing in the studies of East Asian media and cultural connections—the production of knowledge accessible to wider publics and the promotion of people's mediated dialogue—and contrive how to make use of produced knowledge for constructively coordinating the promotion of a sense of sharedness and cross-border dialogue among various social subjects.

This is to take seriously Prasenjit Duara's (2011) reservation with the idea of iteration (as discussed by Spivak) regarding trans-Asian media and cultural flows and connections that, while pluralizing and deessentializing our understanding of the region called Asia, does not turn our attention to interactions and reciprocal connectivity: "We need to recognize our interdependence and foster transnational consciousness in our education and cultural institutions, not at the cost but for the cost of our national attachments" (2011, 982). Indeed, the practice of mutual learning from the experience of other societies and of conversing over transnationally shared issues is a pressing matter, now more than ever, so as to collaboratively tackle the violence of global capital, the rise of various kinds cultural nationalisms, intensifying transnational ethno-cultural flows, and the growing cultural diversity within the nation. Media cultures can play a significant public role—affectively, communicatively, and participatorily—in the promotion of cross-border dialogue over those issues beyond the confinement of the inter-national administration of cultural diversity.

Yet there is no guarantee that mutual learning and cross-border dialogue is enhanced by itself, as we saw in chapters 5 and 6. Resilient forces of guarding national-cultural borders strongly discourage the advancement of such transgressive possibilities. As power configurations of cultural globalization are constantly shifting, ceaseless critical examination of how uneven globalization processes interfere with media and cultural connections in East Asia is essential. Eventually, the situation has been exacerbated. Japan's relationship with China and South Korea has become more antagonistic due to historical and territorial issues. Rejecting dialogue, leaders of the three countries adopt a politically hard line over the issues in order to attract support from the populace. In this context, East Asian media and cultural connections become less noticeable and jingoism and racism has been very conspicuous in Japan, where we have observed the prevalence of aggressive street demonstrations with derogatory racist words against resident Koreans' communities and schools. The development of trans-Asian alliances would be effectual not only to counter the vicious circle of inter-Asian jingoism but also to collaboratively tackle multicultural questions as a shared trans-Asian issue by contesting the structured force that contains them within "national" borders for the administration of cultural diversity. The time is ripe for us to go against such a current by further fostering the new-fangled trans-Asian connection and dialogue via media culture.

The project of "trans-Asia as method" is to envision and materialize East Asia as a dialogic communicative space in which people across borders strive to connect diverse voices, concerns, and problems in various, unevenly overlapping public sites in which the national is still a major site but does not exclusively take over public interests. It aims to transnationally extend our commitment to the local by taking East Asia as a strategic anchoring point. As such, its scope and relevance is cosmopolitan, greatly expanding the regional, and it will be meaningfully achieved only by forming transnational collaborations beyond Japan and Asia. Only such multifaceted, cross-border collaboration would enable us to productively challenge the resilience of exclusionary national-cultural borders toward the actual creation of inclusive social relations and dialogic communicative spaces. And only a sincere and steady endeavor with such an ambitious ideal could lead to the transformation of the real world.

References

Abe, Kiyoshi. 2001. *Samayoeru Nashonarizumu* [Wandering nationalism]. Tokyo: Sekai Shisosha.

Adorno, Theodor W. 1991. *The Culture Industry: Selected Essays on Mass Culture.* Edited with an introduction by Jay M. Bernstein. London: Routledge.

Allen, Greg. 2003. "Interviewing Sofia Coppola about *Lost in Translation.*" *Greg.org: The Making Of,* August 31. greg.org/archive/2003/08/31/interviewing_sofia_coppola_about_lost_in_translation.html.

Allison, Anne. 2006. *Millennial Monsters: Japanese Toys and the Global Imagination.* Berkeley: University of California Press.

Anderson, Benedict. 1983. *Imagined Communities.* London: Verso.

Ang, Ien. 2001. *On Not Speaking Chinese: Living between Asia and the West.* London: Routledge.

———. 2006. "Nation, Migration, and the City: Mediating Urban Citizenship." In "Interaction; Representation and Citizenship," chaired by Johan Fornäs, session 3 of *City and Media: Cultural Perspectives on Urban Identities in a Mediatized World,* edited by Johan Fornäs. Electronically published proceedings of the ESF-LiU conference, Vadstena, Sweden, October 25–29. www.ep.liu.se/ecp/020/.

Ang, Ien, and Jon Stratton. 1996. "Asianizing Australia: Notes toward a critical transnationalism in cultural studies." *Cultural Studies* 10 (1): 16–36.

Anholt, Simon. 2013. "Beyond the Nation Brand: The Role of Image and Identity in International Relations." *Exchange: The Journal of Public Diplomacy* 2 (1): 6–12.

Appadurai, Arjun. 1996. *Modernity at Large: Cultural Dimensions of Globalization.* Minneapolis: University of Minnesota Press.

Aronczyk, Mellisa. 2013. *Branding the Nation: The Global Business of National Identity.* Oxford: Oxford University Press.

Arudou, Debido. *Japanizu onrii* [Japanese only]. Tokyo: Akashishoten, 2003.

Aso, Taro. 2006. "A New Look at Cultural Diplomacy: A Call to Japan's Cultural Practitioners." Speech made at Digital Hollywood University, Tokyo, April 28.

Bauman, Zygmunt. 2001. *Community: Seeking Safety in an Insecure World.* Cambridge: Polity.

Beck, Ulrich. 2006. *Cosmopolitan Vision.* Translated by Ciaran Cronin. Cambridge: Polity.

Benhabib, Seyla. 2002. *The Claims of Culture: Equality and Diversity in the Global Era.* Princeton, NJ: Princeton University Press.

Berry, Chris, Jonathan D. Mackintosh, and Nicola Liscutin, eds. 2009. *Cultural Industries and Cultural Studies in Northeast Asia: What a Difference a Region Makes.* Hong Kong: University of Hong Kong Press.

Bhabha, Homi. 1990. "The Third Space." In *Identity: Community, Culture Difference*, edited by J. Rutherford, 207–21. London: Lawrence and Wishart.

Billig, Michael. 1995. *Banal Nationalism*. London: Sage.

Bunka gaiko no suishin ni kansuru kondankai. 2005. "'Bunkakoryu no heiwa kokka'" nihon no sozo o" [Towards the creation of Japan as a nation of peace and cultural exchanges]. www. kantei.go.jp/jp/singi/bunka/kettei/050711houkoku.pdf.

Calhoun, Craig. *Nations Matter: Citizenship, Solidarity, and the Cosmopolitan Dream*. Oxford: Routledge, 2007.

Carpignano, Paolo, Robin Andersen, Stanley Aronowitz, and William DiFazio. 1990. "Chatter in the Age of Electronic Reproduction: Talk Television and the 'Public Mind.'" *Social Text* 25/26: 33–55.

Carruthers, Ashle. 2004. "Cute Logics of Multicultural and the Consumption of the Vietnamese Exotic in Japan." *Positions* 12 (2): 401–29.

Chakrabarty, Dipesh. 2000. *Provincialising Europe: Postcolonial Thought and Historical Difference*. Princeton, NJ: Princeton University Press.

Chen, Kuan Hsing. 2005. "Asia as Method" [in Chinese with English abstract]. *Taiwan: A Radical Quarterly in Social Studies*, no. 57: 139–218.

———. 2010. *Asia as Method: Toward Deimperialization*. Durham, NC: Duke University Press.

Cho, Hae-Joang. 2005. "Reading the 'Korean Wave' as a Sign of Global Shift." *Korea Journal* 45 (4): 147–82.

Cho, Younghan. 2011. "Desperately Seeking East Asia amidst the Popularity of South Korean Pop Culture in Asia." *Cultural Studies* 25 (3): 383–404.

Chua, Beng Huat. 2004. "Conceptualizing an East Asian Popular Culture." *Inter-Asia Cultural Studies* 5 (2): 200–221.

———. 2010. "Engendering an East Asia Pop Culture Research Community." *Inter-Asia Cultural Studies* 11 (2): 202–6.

———. 2011. "Conceptualization and Inter-referencing." Paper presented at ELLAK (English Language and Literature Association of Korea) International Conference, December 18, Onyang, Korea.

———. 2012. *Structure, Audience and Soft Power in East Asian Pop Culture*. Hong Kong: Hong Kong University Press.

Chua, Beng Huat, and Koichi Iwabuchi, eds. 2008. *East Asian Pop Culture: Approaching the Korean Wave*. Hong Kong: Hong Kong University Press.

Clifford, James. 1988. *The Predicament of Culture: Twentieth-Century Ethnography, Literature, and Art*. Cambridge, MA: Harvard University Press.

Conference of the International and Intercultural Communication Section of the German Communication Association. 2011. Erfurt, Germany, October 27–29.

Consulate-General of Japan in New York. 2004 "'Cool' Japan—Japanese Pop Culture Goes Global." *Japan Info* 11-5 (February/March). www.ny.us.emb-japan.go.jp/en/c/index.html.

Curran, James, and Myung-Jin Park. 2000. *De-Westernizing Media Studies*. London: Routledge.

Curtin, Michael. 2007. *Playing to the World's Biggest Audience: The Globalisation of Chinese Film and TV*. Berkeley: University of California Press.

Delanty, Gerard. 2002. "Two Conceptions of Cultural Citizenship: A Review of Recent Literature on Culture and Citizenship." *Global Review of Ethnopolitics* 1: 60–66.

———. 2007. "Citizenship as a Learning Process: Disciplinary Citizenship versus Cultural Citizenship." *Eurozine*, June 30. eurozine.com/pdf/2007-06-30-delanty-en.pdf.

Duara, Prasenjit. 2010. "Asia Redux: Conceptualizing a Region for Our Times." *Journal of Asian Studies* 69 (4): 963–83.

Erni, John Nguyet, and Siew Keng Chua, eds. 2005. *Asian Media Studies*. London: Blackwell.

Fabian, Johannes. 1983. *Time and the Other: How Anthropology Makes Its Object*. New York: Columbia University Press.

Faiola, Anthony. 2003. "Japan's Empire of Cool; Country's Culture Becomes Its Biggest Export." *Washington Post*, December 27.

Fan, Ying. 2010. "Branding the Nation: Towards a Better Understanding." *Place Branding and Public Diplomacy* 6 (2): 97–103.

Florida, Richard. 2002. *The Rise of the Creative Class: And How It's Transforming Work, Leisure, Community and Everyday Life*. New York: Basic Books.

Fortier, Anne-Marie. 2008. *Multicultural Horizons: Diversity and the Limits of the Civil Nation*. London, Routledge.

Fox, John E. 2006. "Consuming the Nation: Holidays, Sports, and the Production of Collective Belonging." *Ethnic and Racial Studies* 29 (2): 217–236.

Fung, Anthony. 2008. *Global Capital, Local Culture: Transnational Media Corporations in China*. New York: Peter Lang.

Gamson, Joshua. 1998. *Freaks Talk Back: Tabloid Talk Shows and Sexual Nonconformity*. Chicago: University of Chicago Press.

Hafez, Kai. 2007. *The Myth of Globalization*. Cambridge: Polity.

Hagiwara, Shigeru. 2003. "'Kokoga hen dayo Nihonjin': Bunseki wakugumi to bangumi no tokushitsu" ["Kokoga Hendayo Nihonnjin": On the analytical framework and characteristics of the program]. *Media Communication*, no. 53: 5–28.

Hall, Stuart. 1991. "The Local and the Global: Globalization and Ethnicity." In *Culture, Globalization, and the World-System*, edited by Anthony King, 19–39. London: Macmillan.

———. 1992. "The West and the Rest: Power and Discourse." In *Formations of Modernity*, edited by S. Hall and B. Gieben, 275–331. Cambridge: Polity.

Hannerz, Ulf. 1996. *Transnational Connections: Culture, People, Places*. London: Routledge.

Hayashi, Kaori. 2004. "Dorama Fuyu no Sonata no Seijiteki naru mono" [Political aspects of *Winter Sonata*]. *Journal of Information Studies*, no. 69: 56–81.

Hepp, Andreas, and Nick Couldry. 2009. "What Should Comparative Media Research Be Comparing? Towards a Transcultural Approach to 'Media Cultures.'" In *Internationalizing Media Studies: Impediments and Imperatives*, edited by Daya Thussu, 32–47. London: Routledge.

Hesmondhalgh, David. 2008. "Neoliberalism, Imperialism and the Media." In *The Media and Social Theory*, edited by David Hesmondhalgh and Jason Toynbee, 95–111. London: Routledge.

———. 2013. *The Cultural Industries*. 3rd ed. London: Sage.

Hirata, Yukie. 2008. "Touring 'Dramatic Korea': Japanese Women as Viewers of Hanryu Dramas and Tourists on Hanryu Tours." In *East Asian Pop Culture: Analysing the Korean Wave*, edited by Beng Huat Chua and Koichi Iwabuchi, 143–56. Hong Kong: Hong Kong University Press.

Holden, John. 2013. *Influence and Attraction: Culture and the Race for Soft Power in the 21st Century*. London: British Council.

Hu, Kelly. 2004. "Chinese Re-makings of Pirated VCDs of Japanese TV Dramas." In *Feeling Asian Modernities: Transnational Consumption of Japanese TV Dramas*, edited by Koichi Iwabuchi, 205–26. Hong Kong: Hong Kong University Press.

———. 2005. "The Power of Circulation: Digital Technologies and the Online Chinese Fans of Japanese TV Drama." *Inter-Asia Cultural Studies* 6 (2): 171–86.

Huyssen, Andreas. 2003. *Present Pasts: Urban Palimpsests and the Politics of Memory*. Stanford, CA: Stanford University Press.

Ito, Mamoru. 2004. "The Representation of Femininity in Japanese Television Drama of the 1990s." In *Feeling Asian Modernities: Transnational Consumption of Japanese TV Drama*, edited by Koichi Iwabuchi, 25–42. Hong Kong: University of Hong Kong Press.

Ivy, Marilyn. 1995. *Discourses of the Vanishing*. Chicago: Chicago University Press.

Iwabuchi, Koichi. 1994. "Complicit Exoticism: Japan and Its Other." *Continuum* 8 (2): 49–82.

———. 2001. "Uses of Japanese Popular Culture: Media Globalization and Postcolonial Desire for 'Asia.'" *Emergences: Journal of Media and Composite Cultures* 11 (2): 197–220.

———. 2002a. *Recentering Globalization: Popular Culture and Japanese Transnationalism*. Durham, NC: Duke University Press.

———. 2002b. "Soft Nationalism and Narcissism: Japanese Popular Culture Goes Global." *Asian Studies Review* 26 (4): 447–69.

———, ed. 2004a. *Feeling Asian Modernities: Transnational Consumption of Japanese TV Drama*. Hong Kong: University of Hong Kong Press.

———. 2004b. "How 'Japanese' Is Pokémon?" In *Pikachu's Global Adventure: The Rise and Fall of Pokémon*, edited by Joseph Tobin, 53–79. Durham, NC: Duke University Press.

———. 2007. *Bunka no taiwaryoku* [Culture's dialogic capacity]. Tokyo: Nihonkeizaishinbun Shuppansha.

———, ed. 2010. *Tabunkashakai no "bunka" wo tou* [Interrogating "cultural" issues of multicultural society]. Tokyo: Seikyûsha.

Jansen, Sue Curry. 2008. "Designer Nations: Neo-liberal Nation Branding—Brand Estonia." *Social Identities* 14 (1): 121–42.

Jin, Dal Yong, and Lee, Dong-Hoo. 2007. "The Birth of East Asia: Cultural Regionalization through Coproduction Strategies." Paper presented at the annual meeting of the International Communication Association, San Francisco, CA, May 23.

Jung, Sun. 2010. "*Chogukjeok* Pan–East Asian Soft Masculinity: Reading *Boys over Flowers, Coffee Prince* and *Shinhwa* Fan Fiction." In *Complicated Currents: Media Flows, Soft Power and East Asia*, edited by D. Black, S. Epstein, and A. Tokita, 8.1–8.16. Melbourne: Monash University ePress.

———. 2011. *Korean Masculinities and Transcultural Consumption*. Hong Kong: Hong Kong University Press.

Kaneshiro, Kazuki, and Kankurō Kudō. *Go*. Directed by Isao Yukisada. Japan: Toei Company, 2001.

Kaneva, Nadia. 2011. "Nation Branding: Toward an Agenda for Critical Research." *International Journal of Communication* 5: 117–41.

Kawai, Hayao, and Yoneo Ishii. 2002. *Nihonjin to gurôbarizeishon* [The Japanese and globalization]. Tokyo: Kodansha and α-shinsho.

Kayama, Rika. 2002. *Puchi Nashonarizumu Shôkôgun* [Petit nationalism syndrome]. Tokyo: Chûkôshinsho.

Kendall, Gavin, Ian Woodward, and Zlatko Skribs. 2009. *The Sociology of Cosmopolitanism*. London: Palgrave Macmillan Peterson.

Kim, Youna, ed. 2008. *Media Consumption and Everyday Life in Asia*. New York: Routledge.

Klein, Naomi. 2000. *No Logo: Taking Action at the Brand Bullies*. London: HarperCollins.

Kondo, Dorinne. 1997. *About Face: Performing Race in Fashion and Theater*. New York: Routledge.

Koshikawa, Kazuhiro. 2003. Speech at the City University of New York Graduate Center, December 12. www.ny.us.emb-japan.go.jp/en/c/vol_11-5/title_01.html (site discontinued, last accessed March 1, 2004).

Kunihiro, Yôko. 2003. "Gendai Nihon no jendaa hen'you to 'kokoga hen dayo Nihonjin'" [Changing gender relations in contemporary Japan and "kokoga hendayo nihonnjin"]. *Media Communication*, no. 53: 29–48

Kwansai Gakuin University. 2006. Students' presentation at Cultural Typhoon (annual international event), Shimokitazawa, Tokyo, July 1.

Kwok, Jen Tsen, Tseen Khoo, and Chek Ling. 2004. "Chinese Voices: Tseen Khoo, Jen Tsen Kwok and Chek Ling Reflect on the Political Culture of the Asian-Australian Community." *Meanjin* 63 (2): 149–60.

Le, Lan Xuan. 2009. "Imaginaries of the Asian Modern Text and Context at the Juncture of Nation and Region." MA thesis, Massachusetts Institute of Technology.

Lee, Dong-Hoo. 2004. "Cultural Contact with Japanese TV Dramas: Modes of Reception and Narrative Transparency." In *East Asian Pop Culture: Analysing the Korean Wave*, edited by Beng Huat Chua and Koichi Iwabuchi, 157–72. Hong Kong: Hong Kong University Press.

Lee, Ming-tsung. 2004. "Traveling with Japanese TV Dramas: Cross-Cultural Orientation and Flowing Identification of Contemporary Taiwanese Youth." In *Feeling Asian Modernities: Transnational Consumption of Japanese TV Drama*, edited by Koichi Iwabuchi, 129–54. Hong Kong: Hong Kong University Press.

Lee, Paul S.-N. 1991. "The Absorption and Indigenization of Foreign Media Cultures: A Study on a Cultural Meeting Point of East and West: Hong Kong." *Asian Journal of Communication* 1 (2): 52–72.

Liscutin, Nicola. 2009. "Surfing the Neo-Nationalist Wave: A Case Study of Manga Kenkan-ryu." In *Cultural Studies and Cultural Industries in Northeast Asia: What a Difference a Region Makes*, edited by Chris Berry, Jonathan D. Mackintosh, and Nicola Liscutin, 171–93. Hong Kong: Hong Kong University Press.

Livingstone, Sonia, ed. 2005. *Audiences and Publics: When Cultural Engagement Matters for the Public Sphere*. Bristol: Intellect.

Livingstone, Sonia, and Peter Lent. 1994. *Talk on Television: Audience Participation and Public Debate*. London: Routledge.

McGray, Douglas. 2002. "Japan's Gross National Cool." *Foreign Policy*, May–June.

McGuigan, Jim. 2004. *Rethinking Cultural Policy*. London: Open University Press.

———. 2005. "The Cultural Public Sphere." *European Journal of Cultural Studies* 8 (4): 427–43.

———. 2009. *Cool Capitalism*. London: Pluto Press.

Miller, Toby. 2004. "A View from a Fossil: The New Economy, Creative and Consumption—Two or Three Things I Don't Believe In." *International Journal of Cultural Studies* 7 (1): 55–65.

———. 2009. "Can Natural Luddites Make Things Explode or Travel Faster? The New Humanities, Cultural Policy Studies, and Creative Industries." In *Media Industries: History, Theory, and Method*, edited by Jennifer Holt and Alisa Perren, 184–98. Malden, MA: Wiley-Blackwell.

Miller, Toby, Nitin Govil, John McMurria, Richard Maxwell, and Ting Wang. 2005. *Global Hollywood 2*. London: British Film Institute.

Moran, Albert, and Michael Keane, eds. 2004. *Television across Asia: Television Industries, Programme Formats and Globalization*. London: Routledge Curzon.

Mori, Yoshitaka. 2008. "*Winter Sonata* and Cultural Practices of Active Fans in Japan: Considering Middle-Aged Women as Cultural Agents." In *East Asian Pop Culture: Analysing the Korean Wave*, edited by Beng Huat Chua and Koichi Iwabuchi, 127–42. Hong Kong: Hong Kong University Press.

Morley, David, and Kevin Robins. 1995. *Spaces of Identities: Global Media, Electronic Landscapes and Cultural Boundaries*. London: Routledge.

Morris-Suzuki, Tessa. 2003. "Immigration and Citizenship in Contemporary Japan." In *Japan: Change and Continuity*, edited by Javed Maswood, Jeffrey Graham, and Hideaki Miyajima, 163–78. London: Routledge Curzon.

———. 2005. *The Past within Us: Media, Memory, History*. London: Verso.

Nye, Joseph. 1990. *Bound to Lead: The Changing Nature of American Power*. New York: Basic Books.

———. 2004. *Soft Power: The Means to Success in World Politics*. New York: Public Affairs.

———. 2005a. "The Allure of Asia and America's Role." Global Communications Platform, Japanese Institute of Global Communications, December 5. www.glocom.org/opinions/essays/20051205_nye_allure/index.html.

———. 2005b. Interview about Koizumi's visit to Yasukuni Shrine. *Tokyo Newspaper*, October 22.

———. 2005c. "Soft Power Matters in Asia." *Japan Times*, December 5. search.japantimes.co.jp/cgi-bin/eo20051205a1.html.

Okuno, Takuji. 2007. *Japan Cool and Edo Culture*. Tokyo: Iwanami Shoten.

Otsuka, Eiji, and Nobuaki Osawa. 2005. *"Japanimation" wa naze yabureruka* [Why Japanimation should be defeated]. Tokyo: Kadokawa Shoten.

Palmeri, Christopher, and Nanette Byrnes. 2004. "Is Japanese Style Taking Over the World?" *Business Week*, July 26.

Pang, Laikwan. 2006. *Cultural Control and Globalization in Asia: Copyright, Piracy and Cinema*. London: Routledge.

———. 2009. "The Transgression of Sharing and Copying: Pirating Japanese Animation in China." In *Cultural Studies and Cultural Industries in Northeast Asia: What a Difference a Region Makes*, edited by Chris Berry, Jonathan D. Mackintosh, and Nicola Liscutin, 119–34. Hong Kong: Hong Kong University Press.

"Poll: 95% Fear for Japan's Future." 2010. *Asahi Shinbun*, June 12. www.asahi.com/english/TKY201006110455.html.

Robertson, Roland. 1995. "Glocalisation: Time-Space and Homogeneity-Heterogeneity." In *Global Modernities*, edited by Mike Featherstone, Scott Lash, and Roland Robertson, 25–44. London: Sage.

Robins, Kevin. 2000. "To London: The City beyond the Nation." In *British Cultural Studies: Geography, Nationality, and Identity*, edited by David Morley and Kevin Robins, 473–93. Oxford: Oxford University Press.

Roche, Maurice. 2000. *Mega-Events and Modernity: Olympics and Expos in the Growth of Global Culture*. London: Routledge.

Russel, John G. 1991. *Nihonjin no kokujinkan* [The black other in contemporary Japan]. Tokyo: Shinhyouronsha.

Ryang, Sonia. 2000. *Koreans in Japan: Critical Voices from the Margin*. London: Routledge.

Ryoo, Wongjae. 2009. "Globalization, or the Logic of Cultural Hybridization: The Case of the Korean Wave." *Asian Journal of Communication* 19 (2): 137–51.

Said, Edward. 1978. *Orientalism: Western Conceptions of the Orient*. London: Routledge and Kegan Paul.

Salby, Tarik. 2009. "Media and Cultural Studies in the Arab World: Making Bridges to Local Discourses of Modernity." In *Internationalizing Media Studies*, edited by Daya Thussu, 196–213. London: Routledge.

Sassen, Saskia. 2005. "The Repositioning of Citizenship and Alienage: Emergent Subjects and Spaces for Politics." *Globalizations* 2 (1): 79–94.

Sato, Takumi. 2012. "Bunka teikoku "nihon" ni okeru mediaron no hinkon" [Poverty of the discussion of media communication in Japan as a culture nation]. In *Sofuto pawa no media bunka seisaku* [Media cultural policy of soft power], edited by T. Sato, Y. Watanabe, and H. Shibauchi, 143–76. Tokyo: Shin'yousha.

Sawaki, Kotaro. 2004. "Lost in Translation." *Asahi Shinbun*, May 10.

Shattuc, Jane. 1997. *The Talking Cure: TV Talk Shows and Women*. New York: Routledge.

Shim, Doobo. 2006. "Hybridity and the Rise of Korean Popular Culture in Asia." *Media, Culture & Society* 28 (1): 25–44.

Shome, Raka. 2009. "Post-colonial Reflections on the 'Internationalization' of Cultural Studies." *Cultural Studies* 23 (5–6): 694–719.

Silverstone, Roger. 2006. "Media and communication in a globalized world." In *A Demanding World*, edited by C. Barnette, J. Robinson, and G. Milton Keynes Rose, 55–103. London: Open University.

Smith, Michael Peter. 2001. *Transnational Urbanism: Locating Globalization*. Malden. MA: Blackwell.

Sparks Colin. 2007. "What's Wrong with Globalization?" *Global Media and Communication* 3 (2): 133–55.

Spivak, Gayatri Chakravorty. 2008. *Other Asias*. Oxford: Blackwell.

Sreberny-Mohammadi, Annabelle. 1991. "The Global and the Local in International Communications." In *Mass Media and Society*, edited by J. Curran and M. Gurevitch, 118–38. London: Edward Arnold.

Stevenson, Nick. 2003. *Cultural Citizenship: Cosmopolitan Questions*. Maidenhead, UK: Open University Press.

Szondi, Gyorgy. 2008. "Public Diplomacy and Nation Branding: Conceptual Similarities and Differences." Discussion Papers in Diplomacy. The Hague, Netherlands: Clingendael Netherlands Institute of International Relations.

Tai, Eika. 2004. "Korean Japanese: A New Identity Option for Resident Koreans in Japan." *Critical Asian Studies* 36 (3): 355–82.

Takahashi, Nobuyuki. 2001. "Kitty-chan wo tsukutteitanowa dare?" [Who produced Kitty?]. *Shukan Kinyoubi* 357: 56–57.

Takahashi, Toru. 2003. *Japanese Sense of Values and the World Comparison*. Tokyo: Chuko-Shinsho.

Takeuchi, Yoshimi. 2005. "Asia as Method." In *What Is Modernity? Writings of Takeuchi Yoshimi*, edited and translated by Richard F. Calichman, 149–66. New York: Columbia University Press.

Taylor, Charles. 1994. "The Politics of Recognition." In *Multiculturalism and Examining the Politics of Recognition*, edited by C. Taylor and A. Gutmann. Princeton, NJ: Princeton University Press.

Thussu, Daya, ed. 2009. *Internationalising Media Studies*. London: Routledge.

Tobin, Joseph, ed. 2004. *Pikachu's Global Adventure: The Rise and Fall of Pokémon*. Durham, NC: Duke University Press.

Tomlinson, John. 1997. "Cultural Globalization and Cultural Imperialism." In *International Communication and Globalization: A Critical Introduction*, edited by A. Mohammadi, 170–90. London: Sage.

Turner, Graeme. 2003. "After Hybridity: Muslim-Australians and the Imagined Community." *Continuum: Journal of Media and Cultural Studies* 17 (4): 411–18.

———. 2011. "Surrendering the Space: Convergence Culture, Cultural Studies and the Curriculum." *Cultural Studies* 25 (4–5): 685–99.

Urry, John. 2003. *Global Complexity*. Cambridge: Polity.

Utsumi, Aiko, Masataka Okamoto, Shigeo Kimoto, Nobuyuki Sato, and Shinichiro Nakajima. 2000. *Sangokujin hatsugen to zainichi gaikokujin* [Sangokujin speech and foreign nationals in Japan]. Tokyo: Akashi Shoten.

van Ham, Peter. 2001. "The Rise of the Brand State: The Postmodern Politics of Image and Reputation." *Foreign Affairs*, September/October: 1–6.

Varga, Somogy. 2014. "The Politics of Nation Branding: Collective Identity and Public Sphere in the Neoliberal State." *Philosophy and Social Criticism* 39 (8): 825–45.

Vetrovec, Steven. 2001. "Transnational Challenges to the 'New' Multiculturalism." Paper presented at the annual conference of the Association of Social Anthropologist (ASA), University of Sussex, UK, March 30–April 2.

Volcic, Zala, and Mark Andrejevic. 2011. "Nation Branding in the Era of Commercial Nationalism." *International Journal of Communication* 5: 598–618.

Wakabayashi, Mikio. 2005. "Yohakuka suru toshi kukan" [The spread of blank urban spaces]. In *Tokyo Studies*, edited by S. Yoshimi and M. Wakabayashi, 6–25. Tokyo: Kinokuniya Shoten.

Wang, Georgette. ed. 2011. *De-Westernizing Communication Research: Altering Questions and Changing Frameworks*. London and New York: Routledge.

Wilk, Richard. 1995. "Learning to Be Local in Belize: Global Systems of Common Difference." In *Worlds Apart: Modernity through the Prism of the Local*, edited by D. Miller, 110–33. London: Routledge.

Williams, Raymond. 1984. "State Culture and Beyond." In *Culture and the State*, edited by L. Apignanesi, 3–5. London: Institute of Contemporary Arts.

Wimmer, Andreas, and Nina Glick Shiller. 2002. "Methodological Nationalism and Beyond: Nation-State Building, Migration and Social Sciences." *Global Networks: A Journal of Transnational Affairs* 2 (4): 301–34.

Yoda, Tomiko. 2000. "A Roadmap to Millennial Japan." *South Atlantic Quarterly* 99 (4): 629–68.

Yoon, Ae-ri. 2009. "In Between the Values of the Global and the National: The Korean Animation Industry." In *Cultural Studies and Cultural Industries in Northeast Asia: What a Difference a Region Makes*, edited by Chris Berry, Jonathan D. Mackintosh, and Nicola Liscutin, 103–15. Hong Kong: Hong Kong University Press.

Yoshimoto, Mitsuhiro. 1989. "The Postmodern and Mass Images in Japan." *Public Culture* 1 (2): 8–25.

Yúdice, George. 2003. *The Expediency of Culture: Uses of Culture in the Global Era*. Durham, NC: Duke University Press.

Zhao, Yuezhi. 2008. *Communication in China: Political Economy, Power, and Conflict*. Lanham, MD: Rowman and Littlefield.

Index

Adorno, Theodor, 117, 118. *See also*
culture and administration
American cultural influences, 2, 6, 12. *See
also* global cultural power; Hollywood
Ang, Ien, 22, 53, 117; and Jon Stratton,
108
Anholt, Simon, 14, 16
anti-Japanese sentiments in Asia, 34–35,
84
Anti-Korean Wave (*Kenkanryu*), 110
Appadurai, Arjun, 3
Aronczyk, Mellisa, 16–18
Arudou, Debido, 70
Asia as method, 102–103; as mundane
mediated practice, 109, 119. *See also*
inter-Asian referencing; trans-Asia as
method

banal cosmopolitanism, 23, 118
banal inter-nationalism, 4, 6, 9–23. *See
also* banal nationalism; brand
nationalism; inter-national
administration of cultural diversity
banal nationalism, 19
Bauman, Zygmunt, 56
BBC, 34
Beck, Ulrich, 10, 11, 23, 118
Benhabib, Seyla, 9
Billig, Michael, 19
Black Rain, 48, 50

border transgression and cross-border
media and cultural flows, 2–4, 23, 120
Boys over Flowers, 107. *See also Hana
yori dango*; *Meteor Garden*
brand nationalism, viii, 5, 6, 25, 30–40. *See
also* banal inter-nationalism; international administration of cultural
diversity
burden of representation, 73–74

Calhoun, Craig, 116
Carruthers, Ashley, 88–89
Chage and Aska, 85
Chen, Kuan Hsing, 102–103, 119
China: migrants from, 21–22, 37, 56, 70,
72–74; rise of, 21, 26, 36, 100, 102. *See
also* anti-Japanese sentiments in Asia;
history of Japanese colonialism
Cho, Younghan, 105, 108, 112
Chua, Beng Huat, 103–104, 108, 110
Clifford, James, 23
coevalness, 83. *See also* nostalgia
collapse of bubble economy, 26, 49, 54, 82
container model of the nation, 9, 10–11,
13, 19, 20, 53, 118. *See also*
methodological nationalism; national
outlook
cool capitalism, 2
Cool Japan: as cultural policy, 5, 17, 26,
28, 29–32, 36, 38–39, 40; media
discourse of, 26–27; as a Western

About the Author

Koichi Iwabuchi is professor of media and cultural studies and director of Monash Asia Institute, Monash University in Melbourne. His main research interests are cultural globalization and transnationalism, multicultural questions and cultural citizenship, and race/racism and mixed race in Japanese and East Asian contexts. Iwabuchi is the editor of Rowman & Littlefield International's book series Asian Cultural Studies: Transnational and Dialogic Approaches. He is also a coeditor of Hong Kong University Press's book series TransAsia: Screen Cultures. His English-language publications include *Recentering Globalization: Popular Culture and Japanese Transnationalism* (2002); *East Asian Pop Culture: Approaching the Korean Wave* (ed. with Chua Beng Huat, 2008); *Routledge Handbook for East Asian Pop Culture* (ed. with Chris Berry and Eva Tsai, 2015); and *Multiculturalism in East Asia: A Transnational Exploration of Japan, South Korean and Taiwan* (ed. with Kim Hyun Mee and Hsiao-Chuan Hsia, 2015) .